200 cupcakes

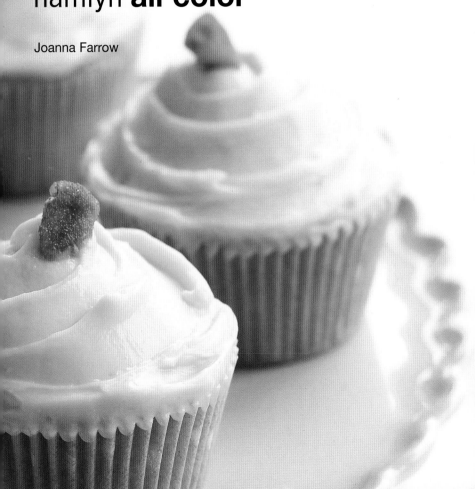

200 cupcakes

hamlyn **all color**

Joanna Farrow

An Hachette UK Company
www.hachette.co.uk

First published in Great Britain in 2010 by Hamlyn,
a division of Octopus Publishing Group Ltd,
2–4 Heron Quays, London E14 4JP
www.octopusbooksusa.com

Copyright © Octopus Publishing Group Ltd 2010

Distributed in the U.S. and Canada by Octopus Books USA:
c/o Hachette Book Group
237 Park Avenue
New York, NY 10017

Some of the recipes in this book have previously
appeared in other books published by Hamlyn.

ISBN: 978-0-600-62098-3

Printed and bound in China

1 2 3 4 5 6 7 8 9 10

Standard level spoon measures are used in all recipes:
1 tablespoon = one 15 ml spoon
1 teaspoon = one 5 ml spoon

The Food and Drug Administration advises that eggs should
not be consumed raw. This book contains some dishes made
with raw or lightly cooked eggs. It is prudent for more vulnerable people, such as pregnant and nursing mothers, invalids,
the elderly, babies, and young children, to avoid uncooked or
lightly cooked dishes made with eggs.

This book includes dishes made with nuts and nut
derivatives. It is advisable for those with known allergic
reactions to nuts and nut derivatives and those who may be
potentially vulnerable to these allergies, such as pregnant and
nursing mothers, invalids, the elderly, babies, and children, to
avoid dishes made with nuts and nut oils. It is also prudent to
check the labels of pre-prepared ingredients for the possible
inclusion of nut derivatives.

contents

introduction

introduction

Cupcakes have become very popular in recent years, and it's easy to see why. Each little cake, with its soft, spongy bottom and sweet topping, provides the perfect-size portion for an indulgent treat. Cupcakes also appeal to both child and adultl. Kids love helping both to make and decorate them, and their enthusiasm for doing so never seems to flag. Conveniently packaged in their mini paper liners, cupcakes are incredibly versatile—ideal for any occasion from an everyday afternoon snack to a special-occasion party. Above all, cupcakes are so effortless to make. While a simple

glaze icing is just the thing for a snack, you may want to try something a little more impressive if you have friends visiting, or if you have a kid's birthday party to cater for or would like to take a selection as a gift or to share, beautifully boxed, when you next visit friends or family.

cupcakes for special occasions

The trend for cupcakes to take the place of a large, traditionally frosted cake for a special occasion is becoming an increasingly favored option. The big bonus here is that they can be attempted by anyone, experienced or beginner, without the need to order them from a specialty supplier. For example, a stunning array of the Wedding Cupcakes on page 224 would look spectacular presented on a tiered cupcake stand (see opposite), while other prettily decorated cupcakes would make an impressive centerpiece for a major birthday, anniversary, or almost any other celebration. Decorations can be as simple as fresh fruit or store-bought sugar flowers, or if you've the time and inclination, sugared fresh flowers (see page 228) or other finishing touches. All look equally impressive. In the book, you will also find seasonal flavors and decorations that are perfectly suited to Christmas, Easter, and Halloween (see pages 204–223).

equipment

Cupcakes require only basic equipment. For most of the recipes, a muffin pan, paper cake liners, and a handheld electric mixer is all that's needed to make a batch of delicious cakes, ready for decorating as simply or creatively as you like.

mini tart pans

These vary slightly, but are usually about the size that you'd use for baking individual jam tarts. The sections generally have sloping sides and are also available with a nonstick coating, which is useful if you're making little cakes without paper liners.

muffin pans

This type of pan has larger, deeper sections with straighter sides, ideal for making larger cupcakes for adult-size portions. Muffin trays are also available with a nonstick coating.

paper cake liner

These come in a vast range of sizes from tiny liners for kids' cakes to giant-size muffin ones. There's also a feast of colors and designs to choose from. Look out for novelty designs for children's birthdays, as well as gold, silver, and colored foils for festive cakes and a rainbow of other hues, from pale pastels to vivid reds. Most of the recipes in this book are designed for a paper liner that's larger than a miniature cupcake liner, but smaller than a muffin one. Use whichever size you prefer, although, of course, if using a

muffin liner where a cupcake liner is called for, you won't make as many, and visa versa. A couple of the recipes in the book use miniature paper cupcake liners, sometimes sold as petit four liners. Pans with tiny holes are available, but you can position the liners directly on a baking sheet.

silicone cups

Brightly colored or pastel silicone cupcake and muffin cups are great for a reliable supply and can be bought in heart or other novelty shapes. Reusable and dishwasher-proof as well as ovenproof, they're easy to use and can be positioned on a baking sheet for cooking rather than in cups in a pan. After use, wash and dry thoroughly before storing.

cutters

Made out of metal or plastic, small cookie cutters, and even smaller cake-decorating cutters in flower or novelty shapes, are great for simple but effective decorations. They range from regular circles to number and letter shapes, animals, stars, moons, trees, and many seasonal motifs. Buy these when you see them and build up a collection in a store you can't find them in the shops when the occasion arises.

cupcake stands

Whether for a birthday party or wedding celebration, piling up cupcakes on a tiered stand looks stunning and eliminates the need for cake cutting. These stands are available in easily assembled cardboard or clear acetate, with pillars or separators to create the layers. Metal cupcake stands that incorporate individual sections to support each cupcake are a good choice for smaller gatherings. Look in kitchen equipment stores or specialty cake-decorating shops, or on the Internet, for a variety of design options.

storing cupcakes

Cupcakes are best served freshly baked. However, if making ahead, they'll keep well in an airtight container for 24 hours, but if keeping them for more than a couple of days, it's best to freeze them, letting them thaw for several hours before decorating. Cakes decorated with buttercream or chocolate frosting, such as the Coffee & Walnut Cupcakes on page 170 or the Chocolate Fudge Cupcakes on page 70, can be frozen already decorated, but those finished with whipped cream or frostings are best decorated once thawed.

some simple techiques

Unlike larger cakes, which are more prone to sinking in the center or being over- or undercooked, there's less that can go wrong when making cupcakes.

mixing the basic sponge

Most of the recipes use the "all-in-one" method in which all the cake ingredients are beaten in a bowl using a handheld electric mixer or using a freestanding electric mixer.

Make sure you've softened the butter beforehand (either gently in a microwave oven or by letting it stand at room temperature) so that the mixture creams together easily. This will take about a minute using the an electric mixer or three to four minutes if you're using a wooden spoon to mix. The ingredients can also be blended together in a large food processor.

making muffins

Muffins are made by folding the "wet" ingredients, such as eggs, melted butter, and buttermilk or milk, into the dry ingredients, including the flour, baking powder, dried fruits, and flavorings. Use a large metal spoon and fold the ingredients gently together until they're only just combined. It doesn't matter if there are traces of flour dispersed in the mixture; overmixing the ingredients will produce a tougher texture.

filling the liners

Cake mixtures rise as they bake, so be careful not to overfill the liners or the mixture will fall over the sides and make the sponge deflate. To avoid this, don't fill the liners more than about two-thirds full. If baking more than 12 cakes, or if you have extra mixture, bake in two separate batches instead of rotating the pans halfway through cooking—as you might with cookies or meringues—because opening the oven halfway through cooking will make the cakes deflate.

testing whether the cakes are cooked

At the end of the cooking time, gently open the oven and lightly touch the top of one of the cakes. The cakes should have risen and the surface should feel soft but not give to the touch. For a basic sponge mixture the crust should be pale golden. Avoid overcooking or the cakes will taste dry.

cooling the cakes

Most of the cupcakes are cooled before decorating. Let them stand in the pan for a couple of minutes once you have taken them out of the oven, then carefully lift them onto a wire rack. Let stand until completely cold before decorating, particularly if using whipped cream or buttercream. Some cakes, including the muffin recipes and savory cupcakes, are best served warm to enjoy their flavor at its best. Muffins don't keep well and any leftovers should be warmed through to refresh them before serving. Ideally, any that are not eaten freshly baked should be frozen for later use.

piped decorations

Certain ingredients, such as whipped cream, meringue, melted chocolate, and buttercream, can be piped onto cupcakes for a more formal, uniform presentation rather than simply spooning or spreading with a knife. Reusable nylon piping bags, available from specialty cake-decorating shops or kitchen stores, can be fitted with a star or plain piping nozzle for piping and then washed ready for reusing. These are good for piping large swirls or decorations onto cakes, such as the Coffee & Walnut Cupcakes on page 170.

For piping scribbled lines or more intricate decorations, such as the Piped Shell Cupcakes on page 30, a paper piping bag is an easier option. These can be bought already made from good cake-decorating suppliers, or you can make your own from triangles of wax paper (see page 16). The advantage of using a disposable bag is that you can have several different bags in use at one time, for example, when using different-colored frostings for decoration. It also means that you can snip off the merest tip of the bag for piping without having to insert a plastic or metal nozzle. Be careful not to snip off too much of the tip, or the frosting will flow out too thick and fast.

making a paper piping bag

Cut out a 10-inch square of wax paper. Fold it diagonally in half. Cut the paper in half, just to one side of the folded line. Holding one piece with the long edge away from you, curl the right-hand point over to meet the center point, making a cone shape. Bring the left-hand point over the cone so the three points meet. Fold the points over several times to secure the cone. Snip off the tip and insert a piping nozzle, if using. Fill the bag halfway and fold over the end to secure.

decorator frosting

Tubes of frosting can be bought in many colors as a quick and easy cake decoration. Some come with changeable tips for piping.

melting chocolate

There are three ways of melting chocolate. When melted with butter or milk, the melting time will be reduced because of the high fat content of these additional ingredients.

To melt on the stove top, chop the chocolate into small pieces and put in a heatproof bowl. Set the bowl over a saucepan of gently simmering water, making sure the bottom of the bowl doesn't come in contact with the water. Once it starts to melt, turn off the heat and let stand until completely melted, stirring once or twice until no lumps remain. It's crucial that no water (including steam) gets into the bowl, or the chocolate will solidify and can't be melted again.

To melt in a microwave oven, chop the chocolate into small pieces and put in a microwave-proof bowl. Melt the chocolate in one-minute spurts, checking frequently. Be particularly careful when melting white or milk chocolate, because they have a higher sugar content and are more prone to scorching.

To melt in the oven, chop the chocolate into small pieces and put in a small ovenproof dish or bowl. Put in the switched-off oven after baking and let stand until melted.

using ready-to-use icing

This soft, pliable icing is available in white or basic colors, or in a wider range of colours from from specialty cake-decorating shops or

suppliers. It can be rolled out on a surface lightly dusted with confectioners' sugar and cut into shapes using cutters or molded like plasticine into shapes. If opening a new slab of ready-to-use icing, knead it lightly to soften it up before rolling out. White icing can be colored by kneading in a few drops of liquid food coloring (to a pastel shade) or paste coloring (for a stronger shade). Any icing that's not in plastic wrap to prevent it from drying out.

using store-bought decorations

These can range from store-bought sugar sprinkles, tiny candies and chocolates to handmade edible flowers available from speciality cake-decorating shops or suppliers. You may want to check the ingredients used in some of the cheaper store-bought decorations before you decide to buy them, or at least use them very sparingly.

frostings

The following favorite frostings are used in several recipes in the book. Alternatively, use them as fillings or toppings for other cupcake recipes of your choice. All three frostings are quick and easy to make, but the chocolate fudge frostings take a little longer, because the chocolate needs to be melted.

buttercream

Makes **enough to generously cover 12 cupcakes**
Preparation time **5 minutes**

10 tablespoons **unsalted butter**, softened
2 cups **confectioners' sugar**
1 teaspoon **vanilla extract**
2 teaspoons **hot water**

Put the butter and confectioners' sugar in a bowl and beat well with a wooden spoon or handheld electric mixer until smooth and creamy.

Add the vanilla extract and hot water and beat again until smooth.

chocolate fudge frosting

Makes **enough to cover 12 cupcakes**
Preparation time **5 minutes**
Cooking time **5 minutes**

3½ oz **bittersweet** or **milk chocolate**, chopped
2 tablespoons **milk**
4 tablespoons **unsalted butter**
⅔ cup **confectioners' sugar**

Put the chocolate, milk, and butter in a small, heavy saucepan and heat gently, stirring, until the chocolate and butter have melted.

Remove from the heat and stir in the confectioners' sugar until smooth. Spread the frosting over tops of cupcakes while still warm.

white chocolate fudge frosting

Makes **enough to cover 12 cupcakes**
Preparation time **5 minutes**
Cooking time **5 minutes**

7 oz **white chocolate**, chopped
5 tablespoons **milk**
heaping 1⅓ cups **confectioners' sugar**

Put the chocolate and milk in a heatproof bowl. Set the bowl over a saucepan of very gently simmering water and let stand until melted, stirring frequently.

Remove the bowl from the pan and stir in the confectioners' sugar until smooth. Spread the frosting over the tops of the cupcakes while still warm.

everyday
cupcakes

vanilla cupcakes

Makes **12**
Preparation time **10 minutes**
Cooking time **20 minutes**

10 tablespoons **lightly salted butter**, softened
⅔ cup **superfine sugar**
1⅛ cups **self-rising flour**
3 **eggs**
1 teaspoon **vanilla extract**

Line a 12-section mini tart pan with paper or foil cake liners, or stand 12 silicone cups on a baking sheet. Put all the cake ingredients in a bowl and beat with a handheld electric mixer for 1–2 minutes, until light and creamy. Divide the cake mixture between the paper or foil liners or silicone cups.

Bake in a preheated oven, 350°F, for 20 minutes, or until risen and just firm to the touch. Transfer to a wire rack to cool.

For cranberry spice cupcakes, make the cake mixture as above, but add ½ teaspoon ground preserved allspice and 1 piece of ginger from a jar, finely chopped, to the cake ingredients before beating. Once beaten, stir in ⅔ cup dried cranberries. Bake as above.

For chocolate cupcakes, make the cake mixture as above, but substitute 2½ tablespoons cocoa powder for 2½ tablespoons of the flour.

fruit & nut cupcakes

Makes **18**
Preparation time **10 minutes**
Cooking time **25 minutes**

10 tablespoons **lightly salted
    butter**, softened
¾ cup packed **light
    brown sugar**
scant 1⅔ cups **self-rising
    flour**
3 **eggs**
1 teaspoon **almond extract**
⅓ cup **chopped mixed nuts**
scant ⅓ cup **mixed dried fruit**

Line two 12-section mini tart pans with 18 paper cake liners. Put the butter, sugar, flour, eggs, and almond extract in a bowl and beat with a handheld electric mixer for 1–2 minutes until light and creamy.

Add the chopped nuts and dried fruit and stir until evenly combined. Divide the cake mixture between the paper liner.

Bake in a preheated oven 350°F for 25 minutes, or until risen and just firm to the touch. Transfer to a wire rack to cool.

For date & orange cupcakes, take scant 1 cup plump, pitted dried dates. Cut 6 lengthwise into thin slices and chop the remainder. Make the cake mixture as above, but use the finely grated rind of 1 orange in place of the almond extract and add the chopped dates instead of the fruit and nuts. Arrange the date slices over the cakes before baking as above.

carrot cupcakes

Makes **12**

Preparation time **20 minutes**,
  plus cooling

Cooking time **25 minutes**

10 tablespoons **lightly salted
  butter**, softened
¾ cup packed **light brown
  sugar**
3 **eggs**
1¼ cups **self-rising flour**
½ teaspoon **baking powder**
1 teaspoon **ground allspice**
1 cup **ground walnuts**
finely grated **zest** of 1 **orange**
1⅓ cups grated **carrots**
⅓ cup **golden raisins**

Frosting
½ cup **whole-fat
  cream cheese**
2¼ cups **confectioners' sugar**
1 tablespoon **lemon juice**
chopped **walnuts**, to decorate

Line a 12-section muffin pan with paper muffin liners. Put the butter, brown sugar, eggs, flour, baking powder, allspice, ground walnuts, and orange rind in a bowl and beat with a handheld electric mixer for about a minute, until light and creamy.

Stir in the grated carrots and golden raisins until evenly mixed. Divide the cake mixture between the paper liners.

Bake in a preheated oven, 350°F, for 25 minutes, or until risen and just firm to the touch. Let stand in the pan for 5 minutes, then transfer to a wire rack to cool.

Beat the cream cheese in a bowl with a wooden spoon until smooth and creamy. Beat in the confectioners' sugar and lemon juice. Spread over the tops of the cakes using a small palette knife and scatter with chopped walnuts to decorate.

For zucchini & hazelnut cupcakes, put 1 scant cup grated zucchini in a small colander. Sprinkle with 2 teaspoons salt and stir together. Put on a plate and let stand for 30 minutes. Rinse thoroughly in several changes of cold water to remove all traces of salt. Pat dry between several sheets of paper towels. Make the cake mixture as above, but use 1 cup ground hazelnuts in place of the ground walnuts and stir in the grated zucchini instead of the grated carrots with the golden raisins. Make the frosting as above and spread over the cakes, then scatter with chopped hazelnuts.

marbled coffee cupcakes

Makes **12**
Preparation time **15 minutes**
Cooking time **20 minutes**

½ cup **lightly salted butter**,
  softened
½ cup **superfine sugar**, plus
  2 teaspoons
2 **eggs**
1¼ cups **self-rising flour**
½ teaspoon **baking powder**
2 teaspoons **espresso coffee
  powder**
1 teaspoon boiling water
½ cup **slivered almonds**,
  lightly toasted
¼ teaspoon **ground
  cinnamon**

Line a 12-section mini tart pan with paper cake liners. Put the butter, the ½ cup sugar, eggs, flour, and baking powder in a bowl and beat with a handheld electric mixer for about a minute, until light and creamy.

Spoon half the cake mixture into a separate bowl. Blend the coffee powder with the boiling water and stir into half the mixture. Using a teaspoon, fill the paper liners with the 2 mixtures, then draw a knife in a circular motion through each cupcake to mix the mixtures partially together to create a marbled effect.

Scatter the slivered almonds over the cakes. Mix the remaining 2 teaspoons sugar with the cinnamon and sprinkle over the cakes.

Bake in a preheated oven, 350°F, for 20 minutes, or until risen and just firm to the touch. Transfer to a wire rack to cool.

For rippled raspberry cupcakes, make the cake mixture as above. Crush ⅔ cup fresh raspberries in a bowl with 2 teaspoons superfine sugar so that they are broken up but not turning to a juicy mush. Fill the paper liners halfway with the cake mixture and flatten with the back of a spoon. Divide the raspberry mixture between the liners and top with the remaining cake mixture. Bake as above and serve dusted with confectioners' sugar.

piped shell cupcakes

Makes **12**

Preparation time **40 minutes**, plus cooling

Cooking time **20 minutes**

1⅔ **confectioners' sugar**, plus a little extra

1–2 tablespoons **lemon** or **orange juice**

12 **Vanilla Cupcakes** (see page 22)

½ quantity **Buttercream** (see page 18)

a few drops of **pink** and **lilac food coloring**

Mix the sugar with 1 tablespoon of the lemon or orange juice in a bowl. Gradually add the remaining juice, stirring well with a wooden spoon, until the icing holds its shape but is not difficult to spread—you may not need all the juice.

Reserve 3 tablespoons of the icing and spread the remainder over the tops of the cooled cakes using a small palette knife. Stir a little extra sugar into the reserved icing to thicken it until it just forms peaks when lifted with a knife. Put in a piping bag fitted with a writing nozzle, or use a paper piping bag with the merest tip snipped off (see page 15).

Color half the buttercream with pink food coloring and the other half with lilac food coloring. Put in separate piping bags fitted with star nozzles.

Pipe rows of pink and lilac buttercream and white icing across the cakes.

For sweetheart cupcakes, press a 1¼–1¾-inch heart-shaped cutter down about ¼-inch into each cupcake and lift out. Scoop out the heart shape. Melt 6 tablespoons strawberry or raspberry jam in a saucepan until softened and spoon into the cavities, spreading it to the edges. Make a small quantity of buttercream by beating together 2 tablespoons softened unsalted butter with scant ½ cup confectioners' sugar and put in a paper piping bag fitted with a writing nozzle. Use to pipe an outline around the edge of each heart shape.

double berry muffins

Makes **12**
Preparation time **10 minutes**
Cooking time **20 minutes**

scant 2½ cups **all-purpose flour**
3 teaspoons **baking powder**
½ cup **superfine sugar**
4 tablespoons **lightly salted butter**
3 **eggs**
4 tablespoons **sunflower oil**
1½ teaspoons **vanilla extract**
⅔ cup **plain yogurt**
⅔ cup **fresh blueberries**
¾ cup **fresh raspberries**

Line a 12-section muffin pan with paper muffin liners. Put the flour, baking powder, and sugar in a bowl and stir together using a fork.

Melt the butter in a small saucepan over a gentle heat and then pour into the dry ingredients. Add the eggs, oil, vanilla extract, and yogurt and stir together until only just combined. Stir in the fresh berries. Divide the muffin mixture between the paper liners.

Bake in a preheated oven, 400°F, for 15 minutes, or until the muffins are well risen and the tops have cracked and turned golden brown.

Loosen the edges of the paper liners with a palette knife to serve warm or transfer to a wire rack to cool.

For juniper & grapefruit muffins, cut away the rind from 2 grapefruit. Working over a bowl to catch the juice, cut the segments from between the membranes. Cut the segments into small pieces. Grind 12 juniper berries with 1 tablespoon superfine sugar as finely as possible in a mortar with a pestle. Make the muffin mixture as above, but omit the berries and add the juniper sugar to the dry ingredients and the grapefruit pieces with the wet ingredients. Bake as above, then drizzle with a glaze made by mixing 2 teaspoons grapefruit juice with heaping ⅓ cup superfine sugar.

lemon & lime drizzle cupcakes

Makes **12**
Preparation time **20 minutes**
Cooking time **35 minutes**

1 **lemon**
2 **limes**
10 tablespoons **lightly salted butter**, softened
scant 1 cup **superfine sugar**
3 **eggs**
1¼ cups **self-rising flour**
½ teaspoon **baking powder**
½ cup **ground almonds**

Stand 12 silicone cups on a baking sheet, or line a 12-section muffin pan with paper liners. Pare thin strips of rind from the lemon and one of the limes using a sharp knife. Slice the pared strips as finely as possible into shreds. Put them in a small saucepan and just cover with cold water. Cook very gently for about 15 minutes, until the shreds are tender—they should be soft enough to break up when squeezed between your thumb and index finger. Drain and let cool.

Squeeze the juice from the lemon and limes.

Put the butter, ⅔ cup of the sugar, the eggs, flour, baking powder, and ground almonds in a bowl. Beat with a handheld electric mixer for about a minute, until light and creamy. Divide the cake mixture between the silicone cups or paper liners.

Bake in a preheated oven, 350°F, for 20 minutes, or until risen and just firm to the touch. Transfer to a wire rack.

Scatter the rind over the cakes while still warm and drizzle with the juice. Sprinkle with the remaining sugar and let cool.

For orange & hazelnut drizzle cakes, pare the rind from 2 small oranges and squeeze 5 tablespoons of orange juice. Shred and cook the orange rind as above. Make the cake mixture as above, but use ½ cup ground hazelnuts in place of the ground almonds. Bake as above. Once cooled, scatter the cakes with the drained orange rind shreds and ¼ cup chopped hazelnuts. Spoon over the orange juice and sprinkle with the remaining sugar as above.

warm pecan caramel cupcakes

Makes **12**
Preparation time **15 minutes**
Cooking time **25 minutes**

½ cup **lightly salted butter**,
    softened
⅔ cup packed **light
    brown sugar**
2 **eggs**
1¼ cups **self-rising flour**
½ teaspoon **baking powder**
1 teaspoon **vanilla extract**
scant 1 cup roughly chopped
    pecans
1 cup **Homemade Caramel
    Sauce** (see right)

Line a 12-section mini tart pan with paper cake liners.
Put the butter, sugar, eggs, flour, baking powder, and
vanilla extract in a bowl and beat with a handheld
electric mixer for about a minute, until light and creamy.

Stir in three-quarters of the pecans and then divide the
cake mixture between the paper liners.

Bake in a preheated oven, 350°F, for 20 minutes,
or until risen and just firm to the touch. Transfer to a
wire rack.

Tip the caramel sauce into a small saucepan and stir
gently over a medium heat until melted but not boiling.
Drizzle the sauce over the cakes while still warm and
scatter with the remaining pecans. You may want
to take the cakes out of their liners to serve.

For homemade caramel sauce, to drizzle over the
cupcakes, put scant 1 cup superfine sugar in a small
saucepan with 5 tablespoons water and heat very
gently, stirring, until the sugar has dissolved. Bring to
a boil and boil rapidly, without stirring, until the syrup
turns to a pale caramel color (watch closely, because
the syrup will quickly overbrown). Remove from the
heat and stir in 4 tablespoons lightly salted butter
and ⅔ cup heavy cream. Return to the heat and cook,
stirring, until smooth.

strawberry cream cupcakes

Makes **12**

Preparation time **30 minutes**, plus cooling

Cooking time **20 minutes**

12 **Vanilla Cupcakes** (see page 22)

2 cups **small fresh strawberries**

⅔ cup **heavy cream**

2 teaspoons **superfine sugar**

½ teaspoon **vanilla extract**

4 tablespoons **red currant jelly**

1 tablespoon **water**

Scoop out the center of each cooled cake using a small, sharp knife to form a deep cavity in each cake.

Hull the strawberries and reserve 6 of the smallest. Thinly slice the remainder.

Whip the cream, sugar, and vanilla extract with a handheld electric mixer in a bowl until just peaking. Spoon a little into the center of each cake and flatten slightly with the back of the spoon.

Arrange the sliced strawberries, overlapping, around the edges of each cake. Halve the reserved strawberries and place a strawberry half in the center of each cake.

Heat the red currant jelly with the water in a small, heavy saucepan until melted, then brush over the strawberries using a pastry brush. Store the cakes in a cool place until ready to serve.

For banoffi cream cupcakes, make and bake the Vanilla Cupcakes as on page 22, but use ¾ cup packed light brown sugar instead of the superfine sugar for the cake ingredients. Slice 2 small bananas and toss in 1 tablespoon lemon juice. Whip ⅔ cup heavy cream with 1 teaspoon vanilla extract until just holding its shape. Place a spoonful on each cooled cake and spread to the edges with the back of a teaspoon. Spoon ½ tablespoon of shop-bought toffee sauce from a jar into the center of each cake and scatter with the bananas. Crush a gingersnap biscuit and scatter a little over each cake.

sultana & ginger cupcakes

Makes **12**

Preparation time **15 minutes**, plus cooling

Cooking time **20 minutes**

4-inch piece of **fresh ginger root**

½ cup **lightly salted butter**, softened

½ cup **superfine sugar**

2 **eggs**

1¼ cups **self-rising flour**

½ teaspoon **baking powder**

½ teaspoon **vanilla extract**

⅓ cup **golden raisins**

1⅔ cups **icing sugar**

several pieces of **candied ginger**, very thinly sliced, to decorate

Line a 12-section mini tart pan with paper cake liners. Peel and finely grate the ginger, working over a plate to catch the juice. Put the butter, superfine sugar, eggs, flour, baking powder, and vanilla extract in a bowl. Add the grated ginger, reserving the juice for the icing. Beat with a handheld electric mixer for about a minute until light and creamy.

Stir in the golden raisins and then divide the cake mixture between the paper liners.

Bake in a preheated oven, 350°F, for 20 minutes, or until risen and just firm to the touch. Transfer to a wire rack to cool.

Beat the confectioners' sugar in a bowl with the ginger juice, making up with enough water to create an icing that just holds its shape. Spread over the tops of the cakes with a small palette knife. Decorate with the candied ginger slices.

For butter-frosted ginger cupcakes, make the cake mixture as above, but use 3 pieces of finely chopped preserved ginger from a jar instead of the fresh ginger and then stir in ¼ cup thinly sliced pitted dried dates in place of the golden raisins. Bake as above. Beat scant ½ cup softened unsalted butter with 7 tablespoons confectioners' sugar and 1 teaspoon hot water until smooth and creamy. Spread over the tops of the cooled cakes and scatter with extra chopped preserved ginger to decorate.

rose delight cupcakes

Makes **12**

Preparation time **15 minutes**,
plus cooling

Cooking time **20 minutes**

4 oz **rose-flavoured Turkish delight**

½ cup **lightly salted butter**, softened

½ cup **superfine sugar**

2 **eggs**

1¼ cups **self-rising flour**

½ teaspoon **baking powder**

1 teaspoon **vanilla extract**

Topping

1¼ cups **heavy cream**

2 teaspoons **rose water**

2 teaspoons **suoerfine sugar**

seeds of 1 small **pomegranate**

Line a 12-section mini tart pan with paper cake liners. Cut the Turkish delight into small pieces using scissors. Put all the remaining cake ingredients in a bowl and beat with a handheld electric mixer for about a minute, until light and creamy.

Stir in the Turkish delight and then divide the cake mixture between the paper liners.

Bake in a preheated oven, 350°F, for 20 minutes, or until risen and just firm to the touch. Transfer to a wire rack to cool.

Whip the cream in a bowl with the rose water and confectioners' sugar until just peaking. Swirl over the tops of the cakes with a small palette knife or pipe through a large star nozzle and scatter with the pomegranate seeds.

For sugar-dusted rose cupcakes, make the cake mixture as above, but omit the Turkish delight. Bake as above. Meanwhile, mix together ¼ cup superfine sugar, 1 tablespoon rose water, and 2 teaspoons lemon juice. Pierce the cooked, still-warm cakes all over with a skewer and drizzle with the sugar mixture until absorbed. Let cool, then generously dust with confectioners' sugar.

very cherry cupcakes

Makes **12**
Preparation time **20 minutes**,
  plus cooling
Cooking time **25 minutes**

⅔ cup **whole blanched
  almonds**
7 tablespoons **lightly salted
  butter**, softened
scant ½ cup **superfine sugar**
2 **eggs**
1 cup **self-rising flour**
1 teaspoon **baking powder**
½ cup **natural candied
  cherries**, quartered
4 tablespoons **cherry or
  strawberry jam**
¾ cup **confectioners' sugar**
2–3 teaspoons **water**
6 **fresh cherries**, halved and
  pitted, to decorate

Line a 12-section mini tart pan with paper cake liners. Put the almonds in a food processor and process until ground.

Tip the ground almonds into a bowl and add the butter, superfine sugar, eggs, flour, and baking powder. Beat well using a handheld electric mixer for about a minute, until light and creamy.

Stir in the candied cherries and then divide the cake mixture between the paper liners.

Bake in a preheated oven, 350°F, for 25 minutes, or until risen and just firm to the touch. Transfer to a wire rack to cool.

Press the jam through a strainer to remove any lumps and spread over the tops of the cakes. Beat the confectioners' sugar in a bowl with the water to make a thick icing that almost holds its shape. Spread a little over each cake and decorate with the cherry halves.

For spicy pineapple cupcakes, make the cake mixture as above, but add ½ teaspoon ground ginger to the other ingredients before beating. Once beaten, stir in ½ cup semidried pineapple, candied into small pieces, in place of the glacé cherries. Bake as above and let cool. Press 5 tablespoons pineapple or ginger jam through a strainer to remove any lumps and brush over the tops of the cakes. Scatter with ¾ cup crushed gingersnaps biscuits and dust with confectioners' sugar to serve.

butterfly cupcakes

Makes **12**

Preparation time **25 minutes**,
   plus cooling

Cooking time **20 minutes**

12 **Vanilla Cupcakes**
   (see page 22)
1 quantity **Buttercream**
   (see page 18)

Cut out a circle from the center top of each cooled cake neatly using a small, sharp knife. Cut each circle in half.

Put the buttercream in a big piping bag fitted with a large star nozzle. Pipe a large swirl of buttercream into the cavity of each cake.

Reposition the 2 halves of the circles on each cake at an angle of 45° so that they resemble butterfly wings.

For vanilla custard butterfly cupcakes, beat together 4 egg yolks, ¼ cup superfine sugar, 1 teaspoon vanilla extract, and 2 tablespoons all-purpose flour in a heatproof bowl. Bring ⅔ cup heavy cream and ⅔ cup milk to a boil in a small saucepan. Pour over the egg yolk mixture, stirring to mix. Return to the pan and cook over a gentle heat, stirring constantly, until very thick. Turn into a small bowl, sprinkle with sugar to prevent a skin from forming, and let cool. Follow the recipe above, but use the vanilla custard instead of the buttercream.

orange & lemon cupcakes

Makes **12**

Preparation time **20 minutes**, plus cooling & setting

Cooking time **15–20 minutes**

4 tablespoons **lightly salted butter**

scant ½ cup **superfine sugar**

2 **eggs**

¾ cup **self-rising flour**

1 tablespoon finely grated **lemon rind**

2 tablespoons **orange flower water**

2–3 tablespoons **milk**

Icing

1⅔ **confectioners' sugar**, sifted

1½ tablespoons **orange juice**

1½ tablespoons **lemon juice**

yellow and **orange food coloring**

finely pared **orange** and **lemon rind coated in superfine sugar**, to decorate

Line a 12-section muffin pan with paper or foil muffin liners. Put the butter, superfine sugar, eggs, flour, and grated lemon rind in a bowl and beat with a handheld electric mixer until smooth.

Add the orange flower water and enough milk to give a good dropping consistency. Divide the cake mixture between the paper or foil liners.

Bake in a preheated oven, 400°F, for 15–20 minutes, or until risen and golden. Transfer to a wire rack to cool.

Slice the risen tops off the cakes. Mix half the confectioners' sugar with the orange juice in one bowl and the other half with the lemon juice in another bowl. Dot a tiny amount of the relevant food coloring into each one and stir well until you have 2 pastel icings.

Pour a small amount of the orange icing over 6 of the cakes, using a teaspoon to cover the surface evenly. Repeat with the remaining cakes, using the yellow icing. Decorate with the sugar-coated orange and lemon rind, pressing it on lightly. Let set completely.

For gooseberry & elderflower cupcakes, make the cake mixture as above, using 2 tablespoons elderflower syrup instead of orange flower water. Bake as above. Thinly slice ⅔ cup gooseberries. Heat in a saucepan with 2 tablespoons water for 2 minutes, until soft. Melt 2 tablespoons gooseberry jam and press through a strainer. Mix with 1 tablespoon boiling water and the gooseberries. Whip ⅔ cup heavy cream with 3 tablespoons elderflower syrup and spread over the cooled cakes. Spoon the gooseberry mixture on top.

honey & banana cakes

Makes **12**

Preparation time **20 minutes**, plus cooling

Cooking time **25 minutes**

1 cup **all-purpose flour**

1 teaspoon **baking powder**

¼ teaspoon **baking soda**

6 tablespoons **lightly salted butter**, melted

heaping ⅓ cup packed **light brown sugar**

2 **eggs**, beaten

2 small, **very ripe bananas**, mashed

Frosting

7 tablespoons **unsalted butter**, softened

5 tablespoons **honey**

5 tablespoons **confectioners' sugar**

dried banana slices (optional)

Line a 12-section mini tart pan with paper cake liners. Sift the flour, baking powder, and baking of soda into a bowl.

Mix together the melted butter, brown sugar, eggs, and mashed bananas in a separate bowl. Tip in the dry ingredients and mix together gently until evenly combined. Divide the cake mixture between the paper liners.

Bake in a preheated oven, 325°F, for 25 minutes, or until risen and just firm to the touch. Transfer to a wire rack to cool.

Beat together the butter, honey, and confectioners' sugar in a bowl until smooth and creamy. Spread over the tops of the cakes using a small palette knife. Decorate with dried banana slices, if liked.

For yogurt & banana cakes, mash 1 large, very ripe banana. Beat together 7 tablespoons softened lightly salted butter and heaping ⅓ cup packed light brown sugar until pale and creamy. Beat in the banana, 1 egg, and ⅔ cup whole-milk yogurt. Sift 1¼ cups self-raising flour and ½ teaspoon baking powder into the bowl and stir in gently. Divide between 12 paper cake liners and bake as above. Transfer to a wire rack and drizzle each cake with 1 teaspoon maple syrup. Serve warm or cold.

rhubarb crumble cupcakes

Makes **12**

Preparation time **20 minutes**,
plus cooling

Cooking time **45 minutes–
1 hour**

sunflower oil, for brushing

9 oz **young rhubarb**, trimmed
and cut into ½-inch lengths

1 cup packed **light brown
sugar**

¾ cup **lightly salted butter**,
softened

1¾ cups **self-rising flour**

1 teaspoon **baking powder**

½ teaspoon **ground cinnamon**

3 **eggs**

3 tablespoons **slivered
almonds**

confectioners' sugar, for
dusting

Line a 12-section muffin pan with paper muffin liners.
Lightly brush a foil-lined baking sheet with oil and
scatter with the rhubarb. Sprinkle with 2 tablespoons
of the brown sugar and bake in a preheated oven,
400°F, for 20–30 minutes, or until tender and beginning
to darken around the edges. Let cool. Reduce the
oven to 350°F.

Put another ¾ cup of the sugar, 10 tablespoons of
the butter, 1⅛ cups of the flour, the baking powder,
cinnamon, and eggs in a bowl and beat with a handheld
electric mixer for about a minute, until light and creamy.
Divide the cake mixture between the paper liners,
spreading it fairly level, and top with the rhubarb pieces.

Put the remaining butter and flour in a food processor
and process until the mixture resembles coarse
bread crumbs. Add the remaining brown sugar and
process briefly until mixed. Scatter over the cakes
and sprinkle with the almonds.

Bake for 25–30 minutes, until risen and golden. Transfer
to a wire rack to cool. Dust with confectioners' sugar.

For raspberry oat crumble cupcakes, make the cake
mixture as above, but replace ¼ cup of the flour with
⅓ cup rolled oats. Divide between the paper liners and
level the tops. Spoon 1 teaspoon raspberry jam into
each case. Put ¼ cup all-purpose flour, ⅓ cup rolled
oats, and 2 tablespoons butter in a food processor
and process until the mixture starts to bind together.
Add 2 tablespoons raw brown sugar and process
briefly until combined. Scatter into the liners, sprinkle
with the slivered almonds, and bake as above.

passion fruit cream cupcakes

Makes **12**
Preparation time **20 minutes**, plus cooling
Cooking time **20–25 minutes**

10 tablespoons **lightly salted butter**, softened
⅔ cup **superfine sugar**
3 **eggs**
1¼ cups **self-rising flour**
½ teaspoon **baking powder**
1 teaspoon **vanilla extract**
4 **passion fruit**
⅔ cup **heavy cream**
¾-1¼ cups **confectioners' sugar**, plus 1 tablespoon

Line a 12-section muffin pan with paper muffin liners. Put the butter, superfine sugar, eggs, flour, baking powder and vanilla extract in a bowl and beat with a handheld electric mixer for about a minute until light and creamy. Divide the mixture between the paper liners.

Bake in a preheated oven, 350°F, for 20–25 minutes, or until risen and just firm to the touch. Transfer to a wire rack to cool.

Halve 2 of the passion fruit and scoop the pulp into a bowl with the cream and 1 tablespoon of the confectioners' sugar. Whip until the cream only just holds its shape.

Peel away the liners from the cakes and split each cake in half horizontally. Sandwich together with the passion fruit cream.

Scoop the pulp of the remaining 2 passion fruit into a bowl. Gradually beat in the remaining confectioners' sugar until you have a thin icing and spread over the cakes.

For peach & red currant cupcakes, make and bake the cakes as above. Let to cool and split horizontally. Whip ⅔ cup heavy cream with 1 tablespoon orange-flavored liqueur or orange juice and spoon over the bottom halves of the cakes. Pile 1 thinly sliced pitted ripe peach and ⅔ cup red currants on top, then add the lids. Dust generously with superfine sugar.

mile-high marshmallow cupcakes

Makes **12**

Preparation time **25 minutes**,
plus cooling

Cooking time **25 minutes**

7 regular **marshmallows**

½ cup **lightly salted butter**,
softened

scant ½ cup **superfine sugar**

2 **eggs**

1¼ cups **self-rising flour**

½ teaspoon **baking powder**

1 teaspoon **vanilla extract**

Topping

11 regular **marshmallows**,
plus extra chopped pieces
to scatter

1¼ cups **heavy cream**

Line a 12-section mini tart pan with paper cake liners. Cut the marshmallows into pieces using kitchen scissors.

Put all the remaining cake ingredients in a bowl and beat with a handheld electric mixer for about a minute, until light and creamy. Stir in the marshmallow pieces and then divide the cake mixture between the paper liners.

Bake in a preheated oven, 350°F, for 20 minutes, or until risen and just firm to the touch. Transfer to a wire rack to cool.

Cut the marshmallows for the topping into small pieces and put about one-third in a small saucepan with half the cream. Heat very gently until melted. Tip into a bowl and let cool.

Whip the remaining cream in a bowl until just holding its shape. Stir in the marshmallow cream and remaining marshmallow pieces, then pile onto the cakes. Scatter with extra chopped marshmallow pieces to serve.

For pink coconut cupcakes, make the cake mixture as above, but add 1 cup dry, shredded coconut to the bowl with the other cake ingredients, use only ¼ cup superfine sugar, and omit the marshmallows. Bake as above. Whip scant 1 cup heavy cream with 1 tablespoon confectioners' sugar until just peaking. Pile onto the cooled cakes and scatter with extra shredded coconut.

plum cornmeal cupcakes

Makes **9**

Preparation time **20 minutes**

Cooking time **20–25 minutes**

mild olive oil or **vegetable oil**, for brushing

1 ⅓ cup **cornmeal**

scant ½ cup **superfine sugar**

1 teaspoon **baking powder**

heaping ¾ cup **ground almonds**

½ teaspoon **almond extract**

⅓ cup **sour cream**

3 tablespoons **mild olive oil** or **vegetable oil**

finely grated **rind** of 1 **lemon**, plus 4 teaspoons **juice**

2 **eggs**

2 **fresh red plums**, pitted and cut into thin wedges

2 tablespoons **honey**

Brush 9 sections of a 12-section muffin pan, preferably nonstick, lightly with oil. Mix together the cornmeal, sugar, baking powder, and ground almonds in a bowl.

Whisk together the almond extract, sour cream, oil, lemon zest, and eggs in a separate bowl until combined. Add to the dry ingredients and mix to a thick paste.

Divide the cake mixture between the cups in the pan and arrange a couple of plum wedges on top of each.

Bake in a preheated oven, 350°F, for 20–25 minutes, or until risen and beginning to color around the edges.

Let stand in the pan for 5 minutes, then loosen the edges with a knife and transfer to a wire rack.

Pierce the tops of the cakes with a skewer. Mix together the lemon juice and honey and drizzle over the cakes while still warm.

For pineapple & coconut cupcakes, put scant ½ cup superfine sugar in a food processor with heaping ¾ cup dry, shredded coconut and process until well blended. Mix with the cornmeal and baking powder as above (omit the ground almonds). Continue to make the cake mixture as above, but use the finely grated rind of 1 lime instead of the lemon. Divide the cake mixture between all 12 cups of the muffin pan and top with thin slices of peeled and cored fresh pineapple instead of the plums before baking as above. Pierce the tops of the cooked cakes with a skewer. Mix 4 teaspoons lime juice with 2 tablespoons honey and drizzle over the warm cakes.

malty raisin cupcakes

Makes **12**

Preparation time **10 minutes**, plus standing

Cooking time **20 minutes**

3 tablespoons **lightly salted butter**, cut into pieces

2 cups **bran flakes**

1 cup **milk**

½ cup **agave nectar** or **light maple syrup**

heaping ¾ cup **raisins**

1¼ cups **self-rising flour**

½ teaspoon **baking powder**

Line a 12-section mini tart pan with paper cake liners. Put the butter and bran flakes in a heatproof bowl.

Bring the milk almost to the boil in a saucepan and pour into the bowl. Let stand for 10–15 minutes, until the bran flakes are very soft and the mixture has cooled slightly, then stir in the agave nectar or maple syrup and raisins.

Sift the flour and baking powder into the bowl and then stir until just mixed. Divide the cake mixture between the paper liners.

Bake in a preheated oven, 350°F, for 20 minutes, or until slightly risen and just firm to the touch. Transfer to a wire rack to cool.

For creamy cinnamon butter, to serve with the cakes, beat 7 tablespoons softened lightly salted butter in a bowl with scant ½ cup confectioners' sugar until light and fluffy. Mix ½ teaspoon ground cinnamon with 2 teaspoons boiling water and add to butter mixture. Beat until evenly combined. Turn into a small bowl and serve with the cupcakes, either piling the butter on top or using to split and fill the cakes.

poppy seed & lemon cupcakes

Makes **12**

Preparation time **20 minutes**, plus cooling

Cooking time **about 1 hour**

2 **unwaxed lemons**

heaping 1 cup **ground hazelnuts**

scant ½ cup **spelt flour**

1 teaspoon **baking powder**

2 tablespoons **poppy seeds**

3 **eggs**

5 tablespoons **agave nectar** or **maple syrup,** plus extra to drizzle

¼ cup **lightly salted butter**, melted

⅓ cup **golden raisins**

Line a 12-section mini tart pan with paper cake liners. Cut one lemon into 12 thin slices. Put with the whole lemon in a small saucepan and cover with boiling water. Simmer very gently for 20–30 minutes, until the slices are tender. Drain the slices and reserve. Cook the whole lemon for another 15 minutes, until soft and squashy. Drain and let cool.

Halve the whole lemon and discard the seeds. Roughly chop, put in a food processor, and process to a puree.

Mix the ground hazelnuts in a bowl with the flour, baking powder, and poppy seeds. Mix the eggs with the lemon purée, agave nectar or maple syrup and melted butter and add to the dry ingredients with the golden raisins. Stir until evenly combined.

Divide the cake mixture between the paper liners and place a reserved lemon slice on top. Drizzle each lemon slice with a little extra agave nectar.

Bake in a preheated oven, 350°F, for 20 minutes, or until risen and lightly browned. Transfer to a wire rack to cool.

For Brazil nut & orange cupcakes, cook 1 small orange as above. Drain, put in a food processor with the eggs, melted butter, agave nectar, or sugar, and golden raisins and process to a puree. Chop and then grind ⅔ cup Brazil nuts. Mix with the flour and baking powder as above, adding ½ teaspoon ground allspice (omit the poppy seeds). Combine with the orange puree mixture and bake as above, with a whole Brazil nut on top of each cake.

iced gingerbread cupcakes

Makes **18**

Preparation time **20 minutes**,
plus cooling

Cooking time **30 minutes**

1¾ cups **all-purpose flour**

2 teaspoons **ground ginger**

1 teaspoon **baking powder**

½ teaspoon **baking soda**

6 tablespoons **lightly salted
butter**, cut into pieces

½ cup packed **light brown
sugar**

scant ½ cup **molasses**, plus
extra to decorate

⅔ cup **milk**

1 **egg**, beaten

heaping ½ cup **mixed
dried fruit**

1¼ cups **confectioners' sugar**

3–4 teaspoons **water**

Line two 12-section mini tart pans with 18 paper cake liners. Put the flour, ginger, baking powder, and baking soda in a bowl.

Put the butter in a small saucepan with the brown sugar and molasses and heat until the butter has melted and the sugar has dissolved. Remove from the heat and stir in the milk, then the egg. Add to the dry ingredients with the dried fruit and mix well. Divide the cake mixture between the paper liners.

Bake in a preheated oven, 325°F, for 25 minutes, or until risen and just firm to the touch. Transfer to a wire rack to cool.

Mix the confectioners' sugar with the water to make a thick icing and drizzle over the cakes. Drizzle thin streaks of molasses over the icing.

For mini oatmeal cupcakes, make the cake mixture as above, but scant ½ cup of the flour with ⅔ cup rolled oats, use ¼ cup mixed dried fruit and add ¼ cup roughly chopped, pitted dried dates or figs, or prunes. Once spooned into the paper liners, sprinkle with extra rolled oats before baking as above. Omit the icing.

breakfast fruit & nut cupcakes

Makes **12**
Preparation time **10 minutes**
Cooking time **15 minutes**

butter, for greasing (optional)
scant 1 cup **rolled oats**
scant 1 cup roughly chopped
  pecans or **walnuts**,
¾ cup roughly chopped
  blanched almonds,
½ cup **slivered almonds**
½ cup **ground almonds**
heaping ¾ cup roughly
  chopped **pitted, dried dates**
⅓ cup **raisins**
5 tablespoons **agave nectar**
  or **maple syrup**

Line a 12-section mini tart pan with paper cake liners, or lightly grease the cups. Lightly toast the rolled oats by stirring them over a gentle heat in a dry skillet. Mix with all the remaining ingredients except the agave nectar or maple syrup in a bowl.

Add the agave nectar or maple syrup and mix well until the ingredients start to bind together—this is best done with your hands. Divide the cake mixture between the paper liners and press down gently.

Bake in a preheated oven, 400°F, for 15 minutes. Transfer to a wire rack to cool.

For spiced apricot & hazelnut cupcakes, make the cake mixture as above, but use ⅔ cup hazelnuts and heaping ¾ cup chopped, plump dried apricots in place of the pecans or walnuts and dates and add ½ teaspoon ground allspice and ½ teaspoon ground cinnamon. Bake as above.

chocolate cupcakes

chocolate fudge cupcakes

Makes **12**
Preparation time **20 minutes**
Cooking time **25 minutes**

½ cup **lightly salted butter**,
  softened
¾ cup packed **light
  brown sugar**
2 **eggs**
¾ cup **self-rising flour**
½ cup **cocoa powder**
½ teaspoon **baking powder**
1 quantity **Chocolate Fudge
  Frosting** (see page 18)

Line a 12-section mini tart pan with paper cake liners. Put the butter, brown sugar, eggs, flour, cocoa powder, and baking powder in a bowl and beat with a handheld electric mixer for about a minute, until light and creamy. Divide the cake mixture evenly between the paper liners.

Bake in a preheated oven, 350°F, for 20 minutes, or until risen and just firm to the touch. Transfer to a wire rack.

Spread the frosting over the tops of the cakes while still warm.

For white chocolate fudge cakes, make and bake the cakes as above. Make 1 quantity of White Chocolate Fudge Frosting (see page 18) instead of the Chocolate Fudge Frosting and swirl over the tops of the cakes while still warm.

chocolate crunchies

Makes **10**

Preparation time **10 minutes**,
plus setting

19 **shortbread cookies**

2 oz **white chocolate**,
chopped

2 oz **milk chocolate**, chopped

8 oz **bittersweet chocolate**,
chopped

2 tablespoons **milk**

6 tablespoons **lightly salted
butter**

1 tablespoon **corn syrup**

chocolate curls, to decorate
(optional)

Line 10 sections of a 12-section mini tart pan with paper cake liners. Put the cookies in a plastic bag and bash with a rolling pin to break up.

Mix the cookie pieces with the white and milk chocolate in a bowl.

Put the bittersweet chocolate in a heatproof bowl with the milk, butter, and corn syrup. Set the bowl over a saucepan of very gently simmering water and let stand until the chocolate and butter have melted, stirring frequently until smooth. Let stand until cool but not beginning to set.

Tip in the cookies and chopped chocolate and mix until coated in the melted chocolate mixture. Divide the mixture between the paper liners and let set. If liked, decorate with chocolate curls and put in ramekins before serving.

For chocolate fruit & nut cupcakes, melt the bittersweet chocolate with the milk, butter, and corn syrup as above, then scatter over ½ cup finely chopped preserved ginger. Let stand to cool but not beginning to set. Sprinkle in ¾ cup chopped walnuts, scant 1 cup chopped, pitted dried dates, and ⅓ cup raisins. Stir gently to mix, then divide the mixture between the paper liners and let set.

chocolate cheesecakes

Makes **6**

Preparation time **25 minutes**, plus cooling

Cooking time **25 minutes**

14 **graham crackers**

1 teaspoon **ground ginger**

3 tablespoons **lightly salted butter**, melted

1 cup **light cream cheese**

heaping ⅓ cup **light brown sugar**

1 **egg**

3½ oz **bittersweet chocolate**, chopped

2 tablespoons **brandy** or **orange-flavored liqueur**

1 tablespoon **water**

⅔ cup **heavy cream**

chocolate curls or **chocolate shards**, to decorate

Put the crackers in a plastic bag and crush with a rolling pin or process in a food processor until crushed. Mix with the ginger and melted butter.

Divide the cracker mixture between 6 double-thickness paper muffin liners and press down firmly with the back of a teaspoon. Place in the sections of a muffin pan.

Beat the cream cheese in a bowl with the sugar and egg. Put the chocolate with the brandy or liqueur and water in a heatproof bowl, set over a saucepan of very gently simmering water, and let stand until melted, stirring frequently until smooth. Stir into the cream cheese mixture and divide between the paper liners.

Bake in a preheated oven, 325°F, for 20 minutes, or until the surface feels lightly set—the cheesecakes will set further as they cool. Let stand in the pan to cool completely.

Whip the cream in a bowl until just holding its shape. Remove the cheesecakes from the paper liners and top with a spoonful of cream. Decorate with chocolate curls or shards.

For chocolate honeycomb cheesecakes, make the cracker mixture as above, but omit the ginger. Divide between the paper liners. Make the cheesecake mixture as above, but reduce the sugar to ¼ cup and use 3½ oz chopped white chocolate instead of the bittersweet chocolate. Once cool, spread with a little whipped cream and scatter with 2 roughly crushed chocolate-covered honeycomb bars.

white chocolate curl cakes

Makes **18**

Preparation time **25 minutes**, plus cooling

Cooking time **25 minutes**

10 tablespoons **lightly salted butter**, softened

⅔ cup **superfine sugar**

scant 1½ cups **self-rising flour**

3 **eggs**

1 teaspoon **vanilla extract**

⅓ cup **white chocolate chips**

3½ oz chunky piece of **white chocolate**

1 quantity **White Chocolate Fudge Frosting** (see page 18)

confectioners' sugar, for dusting

Line two 12-section mini tart pan with 18 paper cake liners. Put the butter, superfine sugar, flour, eggs, and vanilla extract in a bowl and beat with a handheld electric mixer for 1–2 minutes, until light and creamy. Stir in the chocolate chips. Divide the cake mixture evenly between the paper liners.

Bake in a preheated oven, 350°F, for 20 minutes, or until risen and just firm to the touch. Transfer to a wire rack to cool.

Pare curls from the piece of chocolate using a vegetable peeler—if the chocolate breaks off in small, brittle shards, try softening it in a microwave oven for a few seconds first, but be careful not to overheat and melt it. Set the chocolate curls aside in a cool place while frosting the cakes.

Spread the chocolate frosting all over the tops of the cakes, using a small palette knife. Pile the chocolate curls onto the cakes and lightly dust with confectioners' sugar.

For chocolate coconut kisses, make and bake the cakes as above. Let cool. Melt 6 oz white chocolate (see pages 16–17). Transfer one-third of the melted chocolate to a small bowl and stir heaping ¾ cup dried shredded coconut into the remaining larger quantity of melted chocolate. Spread a thin layer of melted chocolate over the tops of the cakes and pile the coconut mixture on top. Let set.

chocolate orange cupcakes

Makes **12**

Preparation time **20 minutes**, plus cooling

Cooking time **25 minutes**

½ cup **lightly salted butter**, softened

½ cup **superfine sugar**

2 **eggs**

1 cup **self-rising flour**

¼ cup **cocoa powder**

½ teaspoon **baking powder**

finely grated **zest** of 1 **orange**

candied orange peel shavings, to decorate (optional)

Frosting

3½ oz **bittersweet chocolate**, chopped

7 tablespoons **unsalted butter**, softened

1 cup **confectioners' sugar**

2 tablespoons **cocoa powder**

Line a 12-section mini tart pan with paper cake liners. Put the lightly salted butter, superfine sugar, eggs, flour, cocoa powder, baking powder, and orange zest in a bowl and beat with a handheld electric mixer for about a minute, until light and creamy. Divide the cake mixture evenly between the paper liners.

Bake in a preheated oven, 350°F, for 20 minutes, or until risen and just firm to the touch. Transfer to a wire rack to cool.

Melt the chocolate (see pages 16–17) and let cool. Beat together the unsalted butter, confectioners' sugar, and cocoa powder in a bowl until smooth and creamy. Stir in the melted chocolate. Pipe or swirl the frosting over the tops of the cakes and decorate with candied orange peel shavings, if liked.

For chocolate prune cupcakes, chop scant ½ cup pitted prunes into small pieces and put in a small bowl with 2 teaspoons brandy. Let soak for 30 minutes. Make the cake mixture as above, stirring in any unabsorbed brandy from the prunes, and divide between the paper liners. Arrange the prunes on top and bake as above. Once cooled, scribble with 1 oz melted bittersweet chocolate.

chocolate peanut cupcakes

Makes **12**

Preparation time **25 minutes**,
  plus cooling & setting

Cooking time **30 minutes**

10 tablespoons **lightly salted butter**, softened

heaping 1 cup **superfine sugar**

3 **eggs**

1¼ cups **self-rising flour**

¼ cup **cocoa powder**

½ teaspoon **baking powder**

⅓ cup **salted peanuts**

3 tablespoons **water**

5 tablespoons **heavy cream**

25 g (1 oz) **unsalted butter**

2 tablespoons **bittersweet chocolate**, chopped

1 tablespoon **corn syrup**

Line a 12-section muffin pan with paper muffin liners. Put the lightly salted butter, ⅔ cup of the sugar, the eggs, flour, cocoa powder, and baking powder in a bowl and beat with a handheld electric mixer for about a minute, until light and creamy. Divide the cake mixture between the paper liners.

Bake in a preheated oven, 350°F, for 20 minutes, or until risen and just firm to the touch. Transfer to a wire rack to cool.

Chop the peanuts finely. Put the remaining sugar in a small saucepan with the water and heat gently until the sugar has dissolved. Bring to a boil and boil rapidly for 4–5 minutes, until the syrup has turned pale golden. Dip the bottom of the pan in cold water to prevent further cooking.

Add ¼ cup of the cream and the unsalted butter to the syrup and heat very gently, stirring, to make a smooth caramel. Stir in the chopped nuts and let stand until cool but not set. Spoon over the cupcakes.

Melt the chocolate with the remaining cream and corn syrup in a small saucepan over a gentle heat. Spoon over the cakes and leave to set.

For chocolate orange cupcakes, make the cake mixture as above, but add the finely grated zest of ½ orange. Bake as above and let cool. Heat 5 tablespoons orange jelly marmalade in a small saucepan with 1 teaspoon water until melted. Let stand until cool but not set. Spread over the tops of the cakes. Melt 3½ oz bittersweet chocolate (see pages 16–17) and spoon over the cakes. Let set.

triple chocolate cupcakes

Makes **12**
Preparation time **30 minutes**,
  plus cooling & setting
Cooking time **25 minutes**

3½ oz **white chocolate**,
  chopped
3½ oz **milk chocolate**,
  chopped
3½ oz **bittersweet chocolate**,
  chopped
3 tablespoons **unsalted
  butter**
12 **Chocolate Cupcakes**
  (see page 22)
cocoa powder, for dusting

Put the white, milk, and bittersweet chocolates in separate microwave-proof or heatproof bowls and add one-third of the butter to each. Melt all the chocolate, either one at a time in a microwave oven or by setting each bowl over a saucepan of very gently simmering water, stirring occasionally until smooth.

Spread the melted white chocolate over 4 of the cakes, using a small palette knife, and dust with a little cocoa powder.

Put 2 tablespoons of the melted milk and bittersweet chocolates in separate piping bags fitted with writing nozzles. Spread the milk chocolate over 4 more of the cakes and pipe dots of bittersweet chocolate over the milk chocolate.

Spread the bittersweet chocolate over the 4 remaining cakes and scribble with lines of piped milk chocolate. Let set.

For double chocolate whirls, make and bake the cake mixture as on page 22, but scatter 3 oz chopped milk chocolate over the mixture in the liners before baking. Once baked, let cool. Whip scant 1 cup heavy cream with 1 tablespoon confectioners' sugar until only just beginning to hold its shape. Put in a piping bag fitted with a large star nozzle and pipe swirls on the tops of the cakes, leaving a dip in the center. Melt 3 oz bittersweet chocolate with 3 tablespoons butter and 1 tablespoon corn syrup and spoon into the centers.

minted white chocolate cakes

Makes **12**
Preparation time **20 minutes**
Cooking time **20 minutes**

5 tablespoons **mint leaves**
scant ½ cup **superfine sugar**
½ cup **lightly salted butter**,
  softened
2 **eggs**
1¼ **self-rising flour**
½ teaspoon **baking powder**
6 oz **white chocolate**,
  chopped
confectioners' sugar, for
  dusting

Line a 12-section mini tart pan with paper cake liners. Put the mint leaves in a heatproof bowl, cover with boiling water, and let stand for 30 seconds. Drain and pat dry on paper towels. Put the leaves in a food processor with the superfine sugar and process until the mint is finely chopped.

Transfer the mint sugar to a bowl and add the butter, eggs, flour, and baking powder. Beat with a handheld electric mixer for about a minute, until light and creamy.

Stir ½ oz of the chocolate and then divide the cake mixture between the paper liners. Scatter with the remaining chocolate.

Bake in a preheated oven, 350°F, for 20 minutes, or until the cakes are risen and just firm to the touch. Transfer to a wire rack to cool. Lightly dust with confectioners' sugar.

For white-chocolate-frosted cardamom cakes, make the cake mixture as above, but omit the mint, simply including the sugar with the other cake ingredients before beating, and add the crushed seeds of 10 cardamom pods. Bake as above and let cool. Heat ⅔ cup heavy cream in a small saucepan until it bubbles up around the edge. Remove from the heat and stir in 5 oz chopped white chocolate. Stir until melted, then turn into a bowl and let cool. Once cool enough to hold its shape when stirred, spoon onto the tops of the cakes and swirl with the back of the spoon.

chocolate strawberry cupcakes

Makes **12**

Preparation time **30 minutes**,
  plus cooling

Cooking time **30 minutes**

¾ cup **cocoa powder**

1 cup **boiling water**

½ cup **lightly salted butter**,
  softened

1⅓ cups packed **light
  brown sugar**

2 **eggs**

1⅔ cups **all-purpose flour**

1 teaspoon **baking powder**

whipped cream, to serve
  (optional)

To decorate

⅔ cup **heavy cream**

4 tablespoons **confectioners'
  sugar**

4 tablespoons **water**

9 oz **bittersweet chocolate**,
  chopped

12 **fresh strawberries**

Line a 12-section muffin pan with paper muffin liners. Put the cocoa powder in a heatproof bowl and mixer in the boiling water. Let cool.

Beat together the butter and brown sugar in a separate bowl until pale and creamy. Gradually beat in the eggs. Sift the flour into the bowl and stir in, then add the cocoa mixture and stir in. Divide the cake mixture between the paper liners.

Bake in a preheated oven, 350°F, for 25 minutes, or until risen and just firm. Let cool in the pan for 10 minutes, then transfer to a wire rack to cool completely.

Put the cream, confectioners' sugar and water in a small saucepan and bring just to a boil. Remove from the heat and stir in 7 oz of the chocolate. Let cool, stirring frequently until smooth and glossy.

Peel away the paper liners and spoon a little of the chocolate mixture over each cake, swirling it slightly down the sides using a small palette knife.

Melt the remaining chocolate (see pages 16–17). Half dip the strawberries in the chocolate and position on the cakes. Serve with whipped cream, if liked.

For chocolate almond sandwich cakes, make the cake mixture as above, divide between the liners and scatter with 3 tablespoons slivered almonds. Bake as above and let cool. Whip ⅔ cup heavy cream with 1 tablespoon confectioners' sugar and 1 tablespoon almond-flavored liqueur. Halve the cakes horizontally and sandwich with the cream. Dust with confectioners' sugar.

warm chocolate brownie cakes

Makes **about 18**
Preparation time **10 minutes**
Cooking time **12 minutes**

3½ oz **milk chocolate**
1 cup **pecans** or **walnuts**
7 oz **bittersweet chocolate**, chopped
10 tablespoons **lightly salted butter**
3 **eggs**
1 cup packed **light brown sugar**
1¼ cups **self-rising flour**
½ teaspoon **baking powder**
cocoa powder, for dusting
ice cream, to serve

Line a 12-section mini tart pan with paper cake liners. Chop the milk chocolate and nuts into small pieces.

Melt the bittersweet chocolate with the butter (see pages 16–17), stirring frequently until smooth.

Beat together the eggs and sugar in a bowl, then stir in the melted chocolate and butter. Sift the flour and baking powder into the bowl and stir in gently.

Stir in the milk chocolate and nuts and then divide the cake mixture between the paper liners.

Bake in a preheated oven, 375°F, for 12 minutes, or until a crust has formed but the cakes feel soft underneath. Let cool in the pan for 10 minutes.

Transfer to plates and top with small scoops of ice cream and a dusting of cocoa powder, if liked. Alternatively, serve cold.

For chocolate blondie cupcakes, chop 7 oz white chocolate into small pieces. Melt another 3½ oz chopped white chocolate with 6 tablespoons butter in a small bowl. Beat together 3 eggs and scant ½ cup superfine sugar in a separate bowl. Stir in the melted chocolate mixture. Sift 1¾ cups self-rising flour into the bowl and stir in gently with ¾ cup chopped blanched almonds and the chopped chocolate. Divide between the paper liners and bake as above.

chocolate toffee cupcakes

Makes **12**

Preparation time **25 minutes**, plus cooling & setting

Cooking time **30 minutes**

½ cup **sweetened condensed milk**

¼ cup **superfine sugar**

5 tablespoons **unsalted butter**

2 tablespoons **corn syrup**

12 **Vanilla Cupcakes** (see page 22)

3½ oz **bittersweet chocolate**, chopped

3½ oz **milk chocolate**, chopped

Put the condensed milk, sugar, butter, and corn syrup in a medium, heavy saucepan and heat gently, stirring, until the sugar has dissolved. Cook over a gentle heat, stirring, for 5 minutes, or until the mixture has turned a pale fudge color.

Leave to cool for 2 minutes, then spoon the toffee over the top of the cooled cakes.

Melt the bittersweet and milk chocolate separately (see pages 16–17). Place a couple of teaspoons of each type of melted chocolate onto a cake and tap the cake on the work surface to level the chocolate. Swirl the chocolates together using the tip of a toothpick or fine skewer to marble them lightly.

Repeat on the remaining cakes. Let the chocolate set before serving.

For mint chocolate cupcakes, mix 1⅜ cups confectioners' sugar with 1 teaspoon natural mint extract and 1–2 teaspoons water in a bowl so that the icing is smooth and just holds its shape. Spread over the tops of the cooled cooked cakes with a palette knife and let stand until lightly set. Melt 3½ oz bittersweet chocolate and spread over the tops of the cakes.

rich fruit chocolate cupcakes

Makes **8**
Preparation time **15 minutes**
Cooking time **35 minutes**

5 tablespoons **lightly salted butter**, softened
⅓ cup packed **light brown sugar**
½ cup **all-purpose flour**
2 tablespoons **cocoa powder**
1 teaspoon **ground allspice**
1 **egg**
heaping ⅓ cup **chopped mixed nuts**
3½ oz **milk chocolate**, chopped
2 tablespoons **candied ginger**, chopped
heaping ½ cup **mixed dried fruit**
raw brown sugar, for sprinkling

Line 8 sections of a 12-section mini tart pan with paper cake liners. Beat together the butter and brown sugar with a handheld electric mixer until pale and creamy. Sift together the flour, cocoa powder, and allspice.

Gradually beat the egg into the butter and sugar mixture, then stir in the flour mixture.

Reserve 2 tablespoons each of the nuts and chocolate and stir the remainder into the cake mixture with the ginger and fruit. Mix well.

Divide the cake mixture between the paper liners. Scatter with the reserved nuts and chocolate and sprinkle with a little raw brown sugar.

Bake in a preheated oven, 300°F, for 35 minutes, or until firm to the touch. Transfer to a wire rack to cool and wrap in extra, decorative paper, if liked.

For apricot & white chocolate cupcakes, make the cake mixture as above, but use an extra 2 tablespoons all-purpose flour instead of the cocoa powder and 1 teaspoon vanilla extract in place of the allspice. Replace the mixed nuts with heaping ⅓ cup finely chopped blanched almonds and the milk chocolate with 3½ oz chopped white chocolate, reserve 2 tablespoons each, and add the remainder to the mixture with heaping ½ cup finely chopped dried apricots instead of the mixed dried fruit (omit the ginger). Spoon the cake mixture into the paper liners with the reserved almonds and white chocolate, sprinkle with a little raw brown sugar, and bake as above.

mocha cupcakes

Makes **12**

Preparation time **15 minutes,** plus cooling & setting

Cooking time **30 minutes**

1 cup **water**

heaping 1 cup **superfine sugar**

½ cup **lightly salted butter**

2 tablespoons **cocoa powder,** sifted

½ teaspoon **baking soda**

2 tablespoons **coffee granules**

1¾ cups **self-rising flour**

2 **eggs,** lightly beaten

Frosting

5 oz **bittersweet chocolate,** diced

10 tablespoons **unsalted butter,** diced

2 tablespoons **corn syrup**

12 **chocolate-covered coffee beans,** to decorate

Line a 12-hole muffin pan with paper or foil muffin liners. Put the water and sugar in a saucepan and heat gently, stirring, until the sugar has dissolved. Stir in the lightly salted butter, cocoa powder, baking soda, and coffee granules and bring to a boil. Reduce the heat and simmer for 5 minutes, then remove from the heat and let cool.

Beat the flour and eggs into the cooled chocolate mixture until smooth. Divide the cake mixture between the paper or foil liners.

Bake in a preheated oven, 350°F, for 20 minutes, or until risen and firm. Transfer to a wire rack to cool.

Put the chocolate, unsalted butter and corn syrup in a heatproof bowl. Set over a saucepan of very gently simmering water and let stand until the chocolate and butter have melted, stirring frequently. Let cool to room temperature, then chill until thickened.

Spread the frosting over the tops of the cakes, decorate each with a chocolate-covered coffee bean, and let set.

For chocolate, rum & raisin cupcakes, soak ⅓ cup raisins in 2 tablespoons rum for about 1 hour until plumped up. Make the cake mixture as above, but omit the coffee granules and add the soaked raisins and any unabsorbed rum with the eggs. Bake and then frost and decorate as above.

chocolate raspberry friands

Makes **10**
Preparation time **20 minutes**
Cooking time **20 minutes**

7 tablespoons **lightly salted butter**
3 oz **bittersweet chocolate**, at room temperature
heaping 1 cup **ground almonds**
½ cup **superfine sugar**
⅓ cup **all-purpose flour**
3 **egg whites**
1¼ cups **fresh raspberries**
confectioners' sugar, for dusting (optional)

Line 10 sections of a 12-section mini tart pan with paper cake liners. Melt the butter in a small saucepan and let cool. Coarsely grate the chocolate—if the chocolate is brittle and difficult to grate, try softening it in a microwave oven for a few seconds first, but be careful not to overheat and melt it.

Mix together the ground almonds, ⅛ cup of the superfine sugar, and the flour in a large bowl. Stir in the melted butter and grated chocolate until just combined.

Mixer the egg whites in a thoroughly clean bowl until peaking. Gradually mixer in the remaining superfine sugar. Using a large metal spoon, fold half the egg whites into the chocolate mixture to lighten it, then fold in the remainder until evenly combined.

Divide the cake mixture between the paper liners and scatter the raspberries on top.

Bake in a preheated oven, 400°F, for 15 minutes, or until golden and just firm to the touch. Transfer to a wire rack to cool. Serve dusted with confectioners' sugar.

For white chocolate blueberry friands, make the cake mixture as above, but use 3 oz white chocolate instead of the bittersweet chocolate. Divide between the paper liners and scatter with ⅔ cup fresh blueberries. Bake as above and let cool. Scatter the cakes with another ½ cup blueberries and drizzle with 2 oz melted white chocolate (see pages 16–17).

chocolate ricotta cakes

Makes **18**

Preparation time **20 minutes**, plus cooling

Cooking time **20 minutes**

10 tablespoons **lightly salted butter**, softened
⅔ cup **superfine sugar**
3 **eggs**
1¼ cups **self-rising flour**
¼ cup **cocoa powder**, plus extra for dusting
½ teaspoon **baking powder**

Filling

8 oz **ricotta cheese**
2 tablespoons **brandy**
⅔ cup **confectioners' sugar**
4 tablespoons **heavy cream**
3½ oz **bittersweet** or **milk chocolate**, chopped
½ cup **slivered almonds**, chopped
¼ cup **natural candied cherries**, chopped

Line 18 sections of two 12-section bun trays with paper cake liners. Put the butter, superfine sugar, eggs, flour, cocoa powder and baking powder in a bowl and beat with a handheld electric mixer for about a minute until light and creamy. Divide the cake mixture between the paper liners.

Bake in a preheated oven, 350°F, for 20 minutes, or until risen and just firm to the touch. Transfer to a wire rack to cool.

Beat together the ricotta, brandy, confectioners' sugar, and cream in a bowl. Gently stir in the chocolate, almonds and cherries.

Cut a thick diagonal slice off the top of each cake and pile the filling onto the cut surfaces. Reposition the slices, twisting them so that the thickest part is uppermost. Serve within 24 hours, dusted with cocoa powder.

For chocolate cream butterfly cupcakes, make and bake the cupcakes as above and let cool. Heat ⅔ cup heavy cream in a small saucepan until almost boiling. Pour into a heatproof bowl and stir in 5 oz chopped milk or bittersweet chocolate. Let stand until the chocolate melts, stirring frequently. Once the cream is cool enough to hold its shape, put in a large piping bag fitted with a star nozzle. Use a sharp knife to cut out a circle from the center top of each cake. Cut the circles in half. Pipe the chocolate cream into the cavities in the cakes. Reposition the 2 halves of circles on each cake at an angle of 45° to resemble butterfly wings. Lightly dust with confectioners' sugar.

frosted choc 'n' nut cupcakes

Makes **12**
Preparation time **20 minutes**,
  plus cooling
Cooking time **20 minutes**

¾ cup **lightly salted butter**,
  softened
scant ½ cup **superfine sugar**
1¼ cups **self-rising flour**
3 **eggs**
heaping 1 cup **ground
  almonds** or **hazelnuts**
2 cups roughly chopped and
  toasted **unblanched
  hazelnuts**
3 oz **white chocolate**,
  chopped
3 oz **milk chocolate**, chopped

Frosting
1 cup **unsalted butter**,
  softened
¼ cup **Vanilla Sugar**
  (see right for homemade)
¾ cup **confectioners' sugar**
2 teaspoons **lemon juice**

Line a 12-section muffin pan with paper muffin liners. Put the lightly salted butter, superfine sugar, flour, eggs, and ground almonds or hazelnuts in a bowl and beat with a handheld electric mixer for 1–2 minutes, until light and creamy.

Reserve a handful of the chopped unblanched hazelnuts for decoration. Add the remainder to the cake mixture with the white and milk chocolates, mix together, and then divide between the paper liners.

Bake in a preheated oven, 350°F, for 20 minutes, or until risen and just firm to the touch. Transfer to a wire rack to cool.

Beat together the unsalted butter, sugars, and lemon juice in a bowl until pale and fluffy. Spread the frosting over the cakes with a small palette knife and decorate with the reserved nuts.

For homemade vanilla sugar, tip 2¼ cups of superfine sugar into an airtight container. Split 2 vanilla beans lengthwise, then cut each in half. Push the vanilla beans down into the sugar and replace the lid. Store in a cool place for at least a week before using, shaking the container frequently to disperse the vanilla flavor. The sugar will keep for several months and can be filled with more sugar and fresh beans when the flavor has reduced.

white chocolate maple muffins

Makes **8**

Preparation time **10 minutes**

Cooking time **20–25 minutes**

scant 2½ cups **self-rising flour**

1 teaspoon **baking powder**

⅔ cup packed **soft brown sugar**

1 **egg**

¼ cup **maple syrup**

1 cup **milk**

¼ cup **lightly salted butter**, melted

4 oz **white chocolate**, chopped, plus extra to decorate

½ cup roughly chopped **pecans**, plus extra to decorate

Line 8 sections of a 12-section muffin pan with paper muffin liners. Sift the flour and baking powder into a bowl and stir in the sugar.

Beat together the egg, maple syrup, milk, and melted butter in a separate bowl and then mix into the dry ingredients until only just combined. Fold in the chocolate and pecans.

Divide the muffin mixture between the paper liners and top with some extra chopped nuts and chocolate.

Bake in a preheated oven, 400°F, for 20–25 minutes, or until risen and golden. Transfer to a wire rack to cool.

For dark chocolate & ginger muffins, finely chop 2 pieces of preserved ginger from a jar. Make the muffin mixture as above, but use 4 oz bittersweet chocolate instead of white chocolate, 3 tablespoons preserved ginger juice in place of the maple syrup and replace scant ½ cup of the flour with ½ cup cocoa powder. Add the chopped ginger with the wet ingredients. Top with extra chopped nuts and bittersweet chocolate and bake as above.

cupcakes
for kids

snakes in the jungle

Makes **12**

Preparation time **55 minutes**, plus cooling

Cooking time **20 minutes**

2 tablespoons **strawberry or raspberry jam**

12 **Vanilla Cupcakes** (see page 22)

6 oz **green ready-to-use rolled fondant**

confectioners' sugar, for dusting

2 oz **red ready-to-use rolled fondant**

2 oz **yellow ready-to-use rolled fondant**

4 **flaked chocolate bars**, cut into 2-inch lengths

2 oz **white ready-to-use rolled fondant**

1 oz **black ready-to-use rolled fondant**

Brush the jam over the top of each cooled cake with a pastry brush. Knead the green fondant on a work surface lightly dusted with confectioners' sugar. Roll out very thinly and cut out 12 circles using a 6 cm 2½-inch cookie cutter. Place a green circle on top of each cake.

Take a small ball of fondant in any color—and roll under the palm of your hand into a thin sausage about 5–6 inches long, tapering it to a point at one end and shaping a head at the other. Flatten the head slightly and mark a mouth with a small, sharp knife.

Roll out a little fondant in a contrasting color thinly and cut out small diamond shapes. Secure along the snake using a dampened paintbrush. Wrap the snake around a length of flaked chocolate and position on top of a cake.

Make more snakes in the same way, kneading small amounts of the fondant together to make different colors, such as red and yellow for orange or red and white for pink. For some cakes, press the chocolate vertically into the cake.

Roll small balls of white fondant and press tiny balls of black icing over them for eyes. Secure to the snakes' heads with a dampened paintbrush.

For multicolored millipedes, cover the cakes with green ready-to-use rolled fondant as above. Arrange a snaking row of mixed licorice candies over each, securing with dots of frosting from a tube of black decorator frosting. Paint small dots for eyes and a smiling mouth on to the front sweet. Pipe tiny legs along the sides of the candies.

alphabetti cupcakes

Makes **12**
Preparation time **45 minutes**,
  plus cooling & setting
Cooking time **20 minutes**

½ cup **lightly salted butter**,
  softened
heaping ½ cup **superfine
  sugar**
2 **eggs**
1¼ cups **self-rising flour**
½ teaspoon **baking powder**
1 teaspoon **vanilla extract**
1¼ cups **white chocolate
  polka dots**

To decorate
3½ oz each of **orange** and **red
  ready-to-use rolled fondant**
  (or use other colors of
  your choice)
confectioners' sugar, for
  dusting
2 oz **white chocolate polka
  dots**, melted

Line a 12-section mini tart pan with paper cake liners. Put the butter, sugar, eggs, flour, baking powder, and vanilla extract into a bowl and beat with a handheld electric mixer for about a minute, until light and creamy. Stir in the polka dots and then divide the cake mixture between the paper liners.

Bake in a preheated oven, 350°F, for 20 minutes, or until risen and just firm to the touch. Transfer to a wire rack to cool.

Working with one color at a time, roll out the fondant on a work surface lightly dusted with confectioners' sugar and cut out small letter shapes using alphabet cutters. Transfer to a tray lined with parchment paper. Reroll the trimmings to make more. Let to set for at least 1 hour, until dry and holding their shape.

Spread each cake with a thin layer of melted chocolate and scatter plenty of letters on top, if necessary securing them to one another with a dampened paintbrush.

For tumbling number cakes, make and bake the cakes as above and let cool. Roll out 3½ oz each of yellow and green ready-to-use rolled fondant on a work surface lightly dusted with confectioners' sugar and cut out numbers using number cutters. Let set and decorate as above.

ladybugs

Makes **12**

Preparation time **40 minutes**,
plus cooling

Cooking time **20 minutes**

2 tablespoons **raspberry** or
strawberry jam

12 **Vanilla Cupcakes**
(see page 22)

6 oz **red ready-to-use
rolled fondant**

confectioners' sugar, for
dusting

4 oz **black ready-to-use
rolled fondant**

½ oz **white ready-to-use
rolled fondant**

small piece of **candied
orange peel**, cut into
matchstick lengths

Brush the jam over the top of each cooled cake.
Knead the red fondant on a work surface dusted with
confectioners' sugar and roll it out. Cut out 12 circles
using a 2½-inch cookie cutter. Place a circle on each one.

Roll out thin strips of black fondant and position one
across each red circle, securing with a dampened
paintbrush. Roll out half the remaining black fondant
to a thin sausage shape, about ½ inch in diameter.
Cut into very thin slices and secure to the cakes to
represent ladybug spots.

Make oval-shaped heads from the remaining black
fondant and secure in position. Roll small balls of the
white fondant for eyes and press tiny balls of black
fondant over them. Secure with a dampened paintbrush.

Press the lengths of candied orange peel behind the
ladybugs' heads for antennae, then press small balls of
black fondant onto their ends. Use tiny pieces of white
fondant to shape smiling mouths.

For busy bees, brush the cooled cakes with jam and
use 6 oz yellow ready-to-use rolled fondant to cover
the cakes as above instead of red fondant. Use
4 oz chocolate-flavored ready-to-use rolled fondant in
place of black icing to shape heads and cut thin strips
to lay across the cakes, securing with a dampened
paintbrush. Add big eyes using a little white ready-to-
use rolled fondant. For the wings, fold small pieces
of rice paper in half and cut out simple wing shapes.
Make a shallow groove on top of each cake (in the
same position as the black strip on the ladybugs)
and gently press the fold into the groove.

frosted banana cupcakes

Makes **12**
Preparation time **25 minutes**,
    plus cooling
Cooking time **20 minutes**

7 tablespoons **lightly salted
    butter**, softened
scant ½ cup **superfine sugar**
2 **eggs**
1 cup **self-rising flour**
½ teaspoon **baking powder**
1 **ripe banana**, mashed
½ cup **golden raisins**
scant ½ cup **whole-milk
    yogurt**
8 oz **confectioners' sugar**
sugar sprinkles, to decorate

Line a 12-section mini muffin pan with paper cake liners. Put the butter, superfine sugar, eggs, flour, and baking powder in a bowl and beat with a handheld electric mixer for about a minute, until light and creamy. Stir in the mashed banana and golden raisins. Divide the cake mixture between the paper liners.

Bake in a preheated oven, 350°F, for 20 minutes, or until risen and just firm. Transfer to a wire rack to cool.

Line a bowl with a double thickness of towels paper. Spoon the yogurt onto the paper. Bring up the edges and gently squeeze out as much liquid as possible. Tip the thickened ball of yogurt onto 2 more sheets of paper towels and squeeze out a little more liquid if possible.

Sift the confectioners' sugar into a separate bowl and add the thick yogurt. Mix well to make frosting with a slightly fudgy texture. Swirl the mixture over the cakes and scatter with sugar sprinkles to decorate.

For clementine cupcakes, make the cake mixture as above, but omit the mashed banana and add the finely grated zest of 2 clementines. Bake as above and let cool. Make the thickened yogurt as above and mix with 4 tablespoons orange curd in a bowl. Swirl over the tops of the cakes and decorate with fresh clementine slices.

on the farm

Makes **12**
Preparation time **55 minutes**,
  plus cooling
Cooking time **20 minutes**

½ quantity **Buttercream**
  (see page 18)
12 **Vanilla Cupcakes**
  (see page 22)
3½ oz **brown ready-to-use
  rolled fondant**
confectioners' sugar, for
  dusting
3½ oz **yellow ready-to-use
  rolled fondant**
3½ oz **pink ready-to-use
  rolled fondant**
½ oz **white ready-to-use
  rolled fondant**
½ oz **black ready-to-use
  rolled fondant**
black food coloring

Spread a thick layer of the buttercream over the cooled cakes. Using a palette knife, lightly peak the fondant on 4 of the cakes.

Knead three-quarters of the brown fondant (wrap the remainder in plastic wrap) on a work surface lightly dusted with confectioners' sugar for the sheep. Reserve a small piece for the ears and roll the remainder into 4 balls. Flatten each ball into an oval shape and gently press onto the cakes thickly spread with buttercream. Shape and position small ears on each sheep.

Reserve a small piece of yellow icing for the ears and roll the remainder into 4 balls for the cows. Flatten into oval shapes as large as the cake tops. Gently press on to 4 more cakes. Shape and position the ears. Use the remaining brown to shape the cows' nostrils and horns, securing with a dampened paintbrush.

Reserve one-quarter of the pink fondant for the pigs' snouts and ears. Roll the remainder into 4 balls and flatten into circles, almost as large as each cake top. Shape and position the snouts and floppy ears, pressing 2 small holes in each snout with the tip of a toothpick or fine skewer.

Use the white and black fondants to make all the animals' eyes—their shape and size to suit each animal. Roll small balls of white fondant and press tiny balls of black fondant over them. Secure with a dampened paintbrush.

Use a fine paintbrush, dipped in the food coloring, to paint on additional features.

Wiggly worms

Makes **11**
Preparation time **45 minutes**,
  plus cooling
Cooking time **20 minutes**

6 tablespoons **unsalted
  butter**, softened
1 cup **confectioners' sugar**,
  plus extra for dusting
12 **Vanilla Cupcakes**
  (see page 22)
2 oz **milk chocolate**, grated
2 oz **pink** or **red ready-to-use
  rolled fondant**
3½ oz **chocolate-flavored
  ready-to-use rolled fondant**
12 small **candy-covered
  chocolate candies**

Beat together the butter and sugar in a bowl until smooth and creamy. Remove one cooled cake from its case and take a thick, angled slice off the top. Spread a little of the buttercream over another cake, position the slice on top and spread with a little more buttercream to make a larger "face" cake.

Spread a large, rectangular board with 4 tablespoons of the buttercream and scatter with the chocolate. Spread the remaining buttercream over the cakes, then position in a snaking line over the chocolate with the face cake at the front.

Roll out the colored fondant thinly on a work surface lightly dusted with confectioners' sugar and cut out 9 circles using a 2-inch cookie cutter. Place on all the cakes except the face and end cakes. Cut out a pointed tail from the trimmings and place on the end cake. Roll out the chocolate fondant and cut out a slightly larger circle. Position on the front cake. Thinly roll out the chocolate fondant and cut out 1-inch circles. Place on the rest of the cakes and top each with a candy-covered chocolate candy. Shape and position eyes and mouth using fondant trimmings and the two remaining candies.

princess cupcakes

Makes **12**

Preparation time **30 minutes**,
   plus cooling

Cooking time **20 minutes**

1 quantity **Buttercream**
   (see page 18)

a few drops of **pink food
   coloring**

12 **Vanilla Cupcakes**
   (see page 22)

edible silver balls

Divide the buttercream between 2 bowls. Add the food coloring to one bowl and mix well. Spread the pink buttercream over the tops of the cooled cakes to within ¼ inch of the edges using a small palette knife, doming it up slightly in the center.

Put half the uncoloured buttercream in a piping bag fitted with a writing nozzle and the remainder in a piping bag fitted with a star nozzle. Pipe lines, ½-inch apart, across the pink buttercream, then across in the other direction to create a diamond pattern.

Pipe little stars around the edges, using the frosting in the other bag. Decorate the piped lines with silver balls.

For jewelled bangle cupcakes, make ½ quantity Buttercream (see page 18). Spread over the tops of the cooled cakes, using a small palette knife. Using a tube of yellow frosting, pipe a circle of icing ½ inch in from the edges of the cake. Arrange a circle of small candies such as candy-covered chocolate drops over the circle. Top each with a dot of frosting and add an edible gold or silver ball.

fruity lunch-box muffins

Makes **12**
Preparation time **10 minutes**
Cooking time **15 minutes**

¾ cup **all-purpose flour**
¾ cup **whole-wheat flour**
2 teaspoons **baking powder**
⅓ cup **superfine sugar**
2 **eggs**
2 tablespoons **mild olive oil**
  or **vegetable oil**
3 tablespoons **lightly salted butter**, melted
2 teaspoons **vanilla extract**
⅔ cup **red fruit yogurt**, such
  as strawberry, raspberry,
  or cherry
¾ cup **fresh raspberries** or
  ⅔ cup **fresh strawberries**,
  cut into small pieces

Line a 12-section mini tart pan with paper cake liners. Put the flours, baking powder, and sugar in a bowl.

Mixer together the eggs, oil, melted butter, vanilla extract, and yogurt with a fork in a pitcher and add to the bowl.

Mix gently with a large metal spoon until the ingredients have started to blend together. Scatter with half the berry pieces and mix a little more until the ingredients are only just combined. Divide the muffin mixture between the paper liners. Scatter with the remaining berry pieces.

Bake in a preheated oven, 400°F, for 15 minutes, or until well risen and just firm. Transfer to a wire rack to cool.

For apple & golden raisin muffins, put 1¼ cups all-purpose flour, ⅔ cup rolled oats, 2 teaspoons baking powder, and ⅓ cup superfine sugar in a bowl and stir in 1 peeled, cored and diced dessert apple and ⅓ cup golden raisins. Mixer together the eggs, oil, melted butter, and vanilla extract as above with ⅔ cup apple- or vanilla-flavored yogurt, add to the dry ingredients, and mix together with a large metal spoon until only just combined. Divide between the paper liners and bake as above.

jelly bean cupcakes

Makes **12**
Preparation time **20 minutes**,
  plus cooling & setting
Cooking time **15–18 minutes**

1¼ cups **all-purpose flour**
⅔ cup **superfine sugar**
12 tablespoons **lightly salted
  butter**, plus extra for greasing
1½ teaspoons **baking powder**
1½ teaspoons **vanilla extract**
2 **eggs**

Icing
1 cup **confectioners' sugar**,
  sifted
½ teaspoon **vanilla extract**
about 4 teaspoons **water**
a few drops of **yellow**, **green**,
  and **pink food coloring**
selection of **jelly beans**,
  to decorate

Line a 12-section mini tart pan with paper or foil cake liners. Put all the cake ingredients in a bowl and beat with a handheld electric mixer for about a minute, until light and creamy. Divide the cake mixture between the paper or foil liners.

Bake in a preheated oven, 350°F, for 15–18 minutes, or until well risen and just firm to the touch. Let cool in the pan.

Mix together the confectioners' sugar, vanilla extract, and enough water in a bowl to make a smooth icing. Divide the icing between 3 bowls and color each batch with a different food coloring.

Remove the cakes from the pan, cover the tops with the different icings, and decorate with jelly beans. Let stand for 30 minutes for the icing to set.

For lemon swirl cupcakes, make the cake mixture as above, but add the finely grated zest of 1 lemon to the other ingredients before beating. Bake as above and let cool. Whip ⅔ cup heavy cream with 1 tablespoon icing sugar until only just holding its shape. Spoon a little over each cake and swirl gently to the edges with the back of a teaspoon. Put a teaspoonful of lemon curd in the center of each cake and scatter with 2–3 finely chopped green jelly candies.

sleepy puppies

Makes **12**

Preparation time **45 minutes**, plus cooling

Cooking time **20 minutes**

½ cup **lightly salted butter**, softened

heaping ½ cup **superfine sugar**

2 **eggs**

1 cup **self-rising flour**

¼ cup **cocoa powder**

½ teaspoon **baking powder**

To decorate

6 tablespoons **unsalted butter**, softened

1 cup **confectioners' sugar**, plus extra for dusting

a few drops of **blue** and **black food coloring**

10 oz **white ready-to-use rolled fondant**

1 oz **black ready-to-use rolled fondant**

Line a 12-section mini tart pan with paper cake liners. Put all the cake ingredients in a bowl and beat with a handheld electric mixer for about a minute, until light and creamy. Divide the cake mixture between the paper liners.

Bake in a preheated oven, 350°F, for 20 minutes, or until risen and just firm to the touch. Transfer to a wire rack to cool.

Beat together the butter and confectioners' sugar in a bowl until smooth and creamy. Beat in the blue food coloring and spread over the cakes using a palette knife.

Take a small portion of the white fondant. Break off a little and reserve for the paws. Shape the remainder into a ball for the head and flatten slightly. Cut the reserved fondant in half and shape 2 paws. Position over the side of one cupcake. Position the head so that it overlaps the paws. Shape 2 floppy ears in black fondant and secure to the head using a dampened paintbrush. Repeat for the remaining cakes.

Use the black food coloring and a fine paintbrush to paint a nose, mouth, eye, patch, and claws over each pup.

For cheeky cats, make and bake the cakes, then cover with the buttercream as above. Shape heads and paws in white ready-to-use rolled fondant as above and position on the cakes. Shape small pointed ears using the white fondant trimmings and secure in place with a dampened paintbrush. Paint eyes, noses, claws, and patches of black markings using black food coloring, then mouths and the centers of the ears with pink food coloring. Cut fine strips of licorice and add for whiskers.

124

ducks, bunnies & chicks

Makes **12**
Preparation time **35 minutes**,
  plus cooling
Cooking time **20 minutes**

1 quantity **Buttercream**
  (see page 18)
a few drops of **yellow** and
  blue food coloring
12 **Vanilla Cupcakes**
  (see page 22)
2 **candied cherries**

Put two-thirds of the buttercream in a bowl and beat in the yellow food coloring. Spread the buttercream in a flat layer over the tops of the cooled cakes, using a small palette knife.

Color the remaining buttercream with the blue food coloring. Put in a piping bag fitted with a writing nozzle, or use a paper piping bag with the tiniest tip snipped off (see page 15).

Pipe simple duck, bunny, and chick shapes onto the buttercream-topped cakes. Cut the candied cherries into thin slices and then into tiny triangles. Use to represent beaks on the ducks and chicks, and tiny eyes on the bunnies.

For Easter chick & egg cakes, make and bake the cakes as on page 22, but add the finely grated zest of 1 lemon to the cake ingredients. Let cool. Beat together 6 tablespoons softened unsalted butter, 1 cup confectioners' sugar, and 2 teaspoons lemon juice until smooth. Spread over the tops of the cakes and position a mini yellow chick and several chocolate mini eggs on each.

pirate faces

Makes **12**

Preparation time **45 minutes**, plus cooling

Cooking time **20 minutes**

2 tablespoons **unsalted butter**, softened

heaping ⅓ cup **confectioners' sugar**, plus extra for dusting

a few drops of **red food coloring**

2 oz **green ready-to-use rolled fondant**

2 oz **white ready-to-use rolled fondant**

12 **Vanilla Cupcakes** (see page 22)

2 oz **black ready-to-use rolled fondant**

small **foil-wrapped chocolate coins**, to decorate (optional)

Beat together the butter and confectioners' sugar in a bowl until smooth and creamy. Beat in the food coloring. Place in a piping bag fitted with a writing nozzle, or use a paper piping bag with the tiniest tip snipped off (see page 15).

Roll out the green fondant on a work surface lightly dusted with fondant sugar. Roll very thin ropes of white fondant and position them about ¼ inch apart over the green fondant. Gently roll with a rolling pin so that the ropes are flattened into the green fondant to create a striped effect. Cut out little semicircular shapes and secure one to each cake to resemble a headscarf, using a little piped red buttercream to secure in place. Use the fondant trimmings to shape knots on one side.

Shape eyes and smiling mouths from white fondant and eye patches and pupils from black fondant. Use the red buttercream in the bag to pipe wiggly lines for hair and around the mouths. Arrange on a plate, scattered with chocolate coins, if using.

For funny clown cakes, beat together 6 tablespoons softened unsalted butter and 1 cup confectioners' sugar until smooth. Thinly spread the cooled cakes with some of the buttercream. Color the remainder with a few drops of yellow food coloring and use to pipe wiggly lines for hair as above. Shape balls of red ready-to-use rolled fondant and position for noses, then add crosses of black ready-to-use rolled fondant for eyes and large smiling mouths in red fondant. Finish with large bowties cut from blue or green ready-to-use rolled fondant.

reindeer cupcakes

Makes 12

Preparation time **40 minutes**, plus cooling & setting

Cooking time **25 minutes**

150 g (5 oz) **bittersweet chocolate**, broken into pieces

1 tablespoon **cocoa powder**

1 tablespoon **boiling water**

4 tablespoons **unsalted butter**, softened

1 cup **confectioners' sugar**

12 **Chocolate Cupcakes** (see page 22)

6 **candied cherries**

1 small packet of **candy-coated chocolate drops**

Melt the chocolate (see pages 16–17). Spoon the melted chocolate into a paper piping bag and snip off the tiniest tip (see page 15). Pipe lines of chocolate about 2½ inches long on a baking sheet lined with nonstick parchment paper. Pipe on small branches for antlers. Make enough for 2 per cake, plus extras in case of breakages. Let stand in a cool place, or refrigerate, to set.

Meanwhile, mix the cocoa powder with the boiling water in a large bowl. Add the butter and then gradually beat in the confectioners' sugar to make a smooth frosting. Spread the frosting over the tops of the cooled cakes. Add a halved cherry for a nose and 2 little sweets for eyes, piping on the remaining melted chocolate to make pupils.

Peel the antlers off the parchment paper and stick at angles into the cakes. Store the cakes in a cool place until ready to serve.

For chocolate snowball cupcakes, make and bake the Vanilla Cupcakes as on page 22, but stir 2 oz chopped white chocolate or chocolate chips into the cake mixture before baking. Beat together 6 tablespoons softened unsalted butter, 1 cup confectioners' sugar and 1 teaspoon boiling water until pale and creamy. Spread over the cooled cakes, using a palette knife, peaking the mixture slightly. Press a white chocolate-covered honeycomb candy into each cake and dust with confectioners' sugar.

fruity flower cupcakes

Makes **12**

Preparation time **30 minutes**,
plus cooling

Cooking time **20 minutes**

½ cup **lightly salted butter**,
softened

heaping ½ cup **superfine
sugar**

2 **eggs**

1¼ cups **self-rising flour**

½ teaspoon **baking powder**

¼ cup finely chopped **semidried pineapple,**

4 tablespoons **smooth
apricot** or **red fruit jam**

scant 1 cup **fruit-flavored
fromage frais**

¼ small **fresh pineapple,**
peeled and cored

½ **mango**, pitted and peeled

handful of **fresh raspberries,
blackberries,** or **pitted
cherries**

handful of **seedless black
grapes**

Line a 12-section mini tart pan with paper cake liners.
Put the butter, sugar, eggs, flour and baking powder
in a bowl and beat with a handheld electric mixer for
about a minute, until light and creamy. Divide the cake
mixture between the paper liners and scatter with the
semidried pineapple.

Bake in a preheated oven, 350°F, for 20 minutes, or
until risen and just firm to the touch. Transfer to a wire
rack to cool.

Spread each cake with a teaspoonful of the jam and
then a thin layer of fromage frais.

Slice the fresh pineapple and mango. Cut circles from
the fruit flesh using a 1-inch cutter and arrange about
5 in a circle over each cake to make a flower shape.
Place a raspberry, blackberry, cherry, or grape in the
center of each, halving if large.

For strawberry cupcakes, make the cake mixture as
above, but use ¼ cup dried strawberries in place of
the semidried pineapple. Bake as above and let cool.
Cut out a circle from the center top of each cake
and spoon a little strawberry jam and strawberry-
flavored fromage frais into each cavity. Reposition
the scooped-out lids on top of the cakes and dust
with confectioners' sugar.

little devils' cakes

Makes **12**

Preparation time **15 minutes**, plus cooling & setting

Cooking time **10–15 minutes**

7 tablespoons **lightly salted butter**, softened

scant ½ cup **superfine sugar**

a few drops of **vanilla extract**

2 **eggs**

¾ cup **self-rising flour**

3 tablespoons **cocoa powder**

8 oz **red ready-use rolled fondant**

about 1 tablespoon **preboiled warm water**

Line a 12-section mini tart pan with paper cake liners. Put the butter, sugar, and vanilla extract in a bowl and beat with a wooden spoon, until light and creamy. Add the eggs and beat the mixture again, then sift in the flour and cocoa powder and stir in. Divide the cake mixture between the paper liners.

Bake in a preheated oven, 350°F, for 10–15 minutes, or until risen and firm to the touch. Transfer to a wire rack to cool.

Put about three-quarters of the fondant in a bowl, add the water and stir until you have a thick but spreadable icing. When the cakes are cool, spread the fondant over the tops with the back of a teaspoon or with a palette knife.

Roll small pieces of the remaining fondant into devil's horns and then position them in the wet icing on top of the cakes. Let stand to set.

For chocolate heart cakes, make and bake the cakes as above. Melt ½ oz milk chocolate with 1 tablespoon butter and 1 tablespoon milk (see pages 16–17). Stir until smooth, then spread over the cakes with a small palette knife. Melt 2 oz white chocolate and pour onto a sheet of nonstick parchment paper. Spread in a thin layer and let stand until set but not brittle. Cut out small heart shapes, using a cutter, and peel away the paper. Position a heart on each cake.

pumpkin heads

Makes **12**
Preparation time **30 minutes**,
  plus cooling
Cooking time **10–15 minutes**

7 tablespoons **lightly salted
  butter**, softened
scant ½ cup **superfine sugar**
a few drops **vanilla extract**
2 **eggs**
¾ cup **self-rising flour**

To decorate
4 oz **red ready-to-use
  rolled fondant**
4 oz **yellow ready-to-use
  rolled fondant**
4 oz **green ready-to-use
  rolled fondant**
4 oz **black ready-to-use
  rolled fondant**
black decorator frosting pen
  (optional)

Line a 12-section mini tart pans with paper cake liners. Put the butter, sugar, and vanilla extract in a bowl and beat with a wooden spoon until light and creamy. Add the eggs and beat the mixture again, then sift in the flour and stir in. Divide the cake mixture between the paper liners.

Bake in a preheated oven, 350°F, for 10–15 minutes, or until risen and firm to the touch. Transfer to a wire rack to cool.

Knead together the red and the yellow fondant to make orange fondant. Roll a little piece of the green fondant into a ball, then flatten into a circle and gently push onto the top of a cake. Roll a larger piece of the orange fondant into a ball. Place on top of the green "pumpkin patch". Roll a tiny piece of green fondant into a stalk and push onto the top of the orange pumpkin. Use the black fondant to make eyes and a crooked smile. Alternatively, draw the features onto the pumpkin head with a black decorator pen.

For fall leaf cakes, make and bake the cakes as above. Beat together 6 tablespoons softened unsalted butter, 1 cup confectioners' sugar, 1 teaspoon boiling water, and a few drops of green food coloring. Spread over the cooled cakes, peaking with the back of a teaspoon. Roll 3 oz each of chocolate-flavored, light brown, and yellow ready-to-use rolled fondant out thinly on a work surface lightly dusted with confectioners' sugar and cut out small leaf shapes, using a knife or cutter. Mark veins with a knife and arrange over and around the cakes, bending them slightly so that they set in curved shapes.

birthday cake stack

Makes **18**
Preparation time **25 minutes**,
  plus cooling
Cooking time **20 minutes**

¾ cup **lightly salted butter**,
  softened
¾ cup **superfine sugar**
3 **eggs**
1⅔ cups **self-rising flour**
1 teaspoon **baking powder**
finely grated **zest** of 2 **lemons**

To decorate
½ cup **unsalted butter**,
  softened
1⅔ cups **confectioners' sugar**
a few drops of **pink** or **blue**
  food coloring
4 oz small **candies**, such as
  licorice mixtures and jellies
sugar sprinkles (optional)
birthday candles and
  candleholders

Line 18 sections of two 12-section mini tart pans with paper cake liners. Put all the cake ingredients in a bowl and beat with a handheld electric mixer for about a minute, until light and creamy. Divide the cake mixture between the paper liners.

Bake in a preheated oven, 350°F, for 20 minutes, or until risen and just firm to the touch. Transfer to a wire rack to cool.

Beat together the unsalted butter and confectioners' sugar in a bowl until smooth and creamy. Beat in the food coloring. Spread the buttercream over the cooled cakes, using a small palette knife. Decorate the cakes with plenty of small candles and sugar sprinkles, if using.

Arrange a layer of cakes on a serving plate and stack another 2 or 3 tiers on top. Push the required amount of birthday candles and candleholders into the cakes.

For chocolate cake stack, make the cake mixture as above, but use heaping ⅓ cup cocoa powder in place of ⅓ cup of the flour. Bake as above. Beat together ½ cup softened unsalted butter and 1⅔ cups confectioners' sugar until smooth. Blend heaping ⅓ cup cocoa powder with 5 tablespoons boiling water and beat into the buttercream mixture. Spread over the cooled cakes. Scatter the cakes with small chocolate candies, such as chopped chocolate-covered honeycomb, candy-covered chocolate drops, and chocolate polka dots. Scatter with chocolate sprinkles before stacking as above.

number cakes

Makes **12**
Preparation time **25 minutes**,
plus cooling
Cooking time **20 minutes**

a few drops of **green** or
yellow food coloring
1 quantity **Buttercream**
(see page 18)
12 **Vanilla Cupcakes**
(see page 22)
6 oz **white ready-to-use
rolled fondant**
confectioners' sugar, for
dusting
2 oz **red ready-to-use
rolled fondant**
2 oz **blue ready-to-use
rolled fondant**
colored sugar strands

Beat the food coloring into the buttercream and then spread all over the tops of the cooled cakes, using a small palette knife.

Knead the white fondant on a work surface lightly dusted with confectioners' sugar, then roll out. Cut out 12 circles using a 2½-inch cookie cutter and gently press one onto the top of each cake.

Roll out the red fondant and cut out numbers of your choice for 6 of the cakes, using a small, sharp knife or alphabet cutters. Secure to the cakes with a dampened paintbrush. Cut out the remaining numbers from the blue fondant.

Brush the edges of the white fondant with a dampened paintbrush and scatter over the sugar strands.

For party "name" cakes, make the buttercream as above, omitting the food coloring, and reserve 4 tablespoons. Spread the remainder over the cooled cakes, smoothing it as flat as possible with a small palette knife. Color the reserved buttercream with a few drops of red food coloring (or a color of your choice), put in a paper piping bag, and snip off the tiniest tip (see page 15). Pipe names or initials over the cakes. Put several clear boiled candies in a plastic bag and crush with a rolling pin. Scatter around the edges of the cakes.

cupcakes
for adults

marsala raisin & ricotta cakes

Makes **12**

Preparation time **20 minutes**,
  plus cooling

Cooking time **25 minutes**

⅔ cup **raisins**

5 tablespoons **Marsala** or
  dry sherry

½ cup **lightly salted butter**,
  softened

½ cup packed **light brown
  sugar**

1 teaspoon **vanilla extract**

2 **eggs**

1¼ cups **self-rising flour**

½ teaspoon **baking powder**

Frosting

1 cup **ricotta cheese**

heaping ⅓ **confectioners'
  sugar**

To decorate

handful of **slivered almonds**,
  lightly toasted

12 **raisins**

Line a 12-section mini tart pan with paper cake liners. Put the raisins in a small saucepan with the Marsala or sherry and heat until bubbling around the edge. Simmer for 1 minute, then remove from the heat and turn into a bowl. Let cool.

Put the butter, brown sugar, vanilla extract, eggs, flour, and baking powder in a separate bowl and beat with a handheld electric mixer for about a minute, until light and creamy.

Drain the raisins thoroughly, reserving the unabsorbed Marsala or sherry, and stir into the cake mixture. Divide between the cake liners.

Bake in a preheated oven, 350°F, for 20 minutes, or until risen and just firm. Transfer to a wire rack to cool.

Put the ricotta in a bowl and gently stir in 1 teaspoon of the reserved Marsala or sherry and the confectioners' sugar—don't overbeat the mixture or it will become too runny.

Pierce the tops of the cakes with a skewer and drizzle with the remaining Marsala or sherry. Spread the ricotta mixture on top. Use the slivered almonds and raisins to decorate each cake with a simple flower shape.

For rum & raisin cheesecakes, soak ⅔ cup raisins in 3 tablespoons rum for several hours, until absorbed. Make the cake mixture as above, but replace the Marsala or sherry-soaked raisins with the rum-soaked raisins. Bake as above. Beat scant 1 cup cream cheese with ⅓ cup confectioners' sugar and spread over the cakes. Scatter with crushed graham crackers.

hot & spicy cupcakes

Makes **12**

Preparation time **15 minutes**, plus cooling

Cooking time **25 minutes**

1 **medium-strength red chile**, seeded and finely chopped, plus 6 small **red chiles**, halved lengthwise

½ cup **lightly salted butter**, softened

¾ cup **superfine sugar**

2 **eggs**

1¼ cups **self-rising flour**

½ teaspoon **baking powder**

1 cup chopped, **soft dried mango**,

2 tablespoons **water**

5 tablespoons **vodka**

⅔ cup **confectioners' sugar**

finely grated **zest** of 1 **lime**, to sprinkle

Line a 12-section mini tart pan with paper cake liners. Put the chopped chile, butter, ½ cup of the superfine sugar, the eggs, flour, and baking powder in a bowl and beat with a handheld electric mixer for about a minute, until light and creamy.

Stir in the mango and then divide the cake mixture between the paper liners. Place a halved chile across the top of each cake.

Bake in a preheated oven, 350°F, for 20 minutes, or until risen and just firm to the touch. Transfer to a wire rack to cool.

Put the remaining superfine sugar in a small saucepan with the water and heat gently until the sugar has dissolved. Bring to a boil and boil for 3–4 minutes, until thickened and syrupy. Stir in 4 tablespoons of the vodka (be careful because the mixture will splutter) and heat until smooth.

Pierce the tops of the cakes with a skewer and drizzle the syrup over. Blend the remaining vodka with the confectioners' sugar to make a thin paste and drizzle over the cakes. Sprinkle with the lime zest.

For iced fresh ginger cupcakes, peel and finely grate a 4-inch piece fresh ginger root, working over a bowl to catch the juice. Make the cake mixture as above, adding the grated ginger in place of the chopped chile, reserving the ginger juice. Bake as above. Once the cakes are cool, mix the ginger juice with ⅔ cup confectioners' sugar to make a thin glaze, adding a dash of lemon juice if the mixture is too dry. Use to decorate the cakes.

almond praline cupcakes

Makes **12**

Preparation time **30 minutes**,
  plus cooling

Cooking time **25 minutes**

sunflower oil, for brushing

heaping 1 cup **superfine
  sugar**

scant ½ cup **water**

¾ cup **slivered almonds**

½ cup **lightly salted butter**,
  softened

1 teaspoon **vanilla extract**

2 **eggs**

1¼ cups **self-rising flour**

½ teaspoon **baking powder**

Frosting

6 tablespoons **unsalted
  butter**, softened

1 cup **confectioners' sugar**

1 teaspoon **hot water**

Line a 12-section mini tart pan with paper cake liners. Brush a baking sheet lightly with oil. Put ⅔ cup of the superfine sugar in a small, heavy saucepan with the water and heat gently until it has dissolved. Bring to a boil and boil rapidly until the syrup has turned to a pale golden caramel. Immediately stir in the slivered almonds. When coated, turn out on to the prepared baking sheet, spread in a thin layer, and let stand until cold and brittle.

Snap half the praline into jagged pieces and reserve. Process the remainder in a food processor until ground.

Put the butter, remaining superfine sugar, vanilla extract, eggs, flour, and baking powder in a bowl and beat with a handheld electric mixer for about a minute, until light and creamy. Stir in the ground praline. Divide the cake mixture between the paper liners.

Bake in a preheated oven, 350°F, for 20 minutes, or until risen and just firm to the touch. Transfer to a wire rack to cool.

Beat together the butter and confectioners' sugar with the hot water in a bowl until pale and creamy. Spread over the cakes, using a small palette knife. Decorate with the praline pieces.

For maple & pecan praline cakes, make the praline as above, but use scant ¾ cup pecans instead of the almonds. Grind half the praline in a food processor. Make the cake mixture as above, adding the ground pecan praline. Bake as above. Whip ⅔ cup heavy cream with 3 tablespoons maple syrup until just holding its shape. Spoon over the cooled cakes. Scatter with the praline pieces.

strawberry marguerita cupcakes

Makes **12**

Preparation time **25 minutes**, plus soaking & cooling

Cooking time **20 minutes**

½ cup **dried strawberries**

6 tablespoons **tequila**

½ cup **lightly salted butter**, softened

heaping ½ cup **superfine sugar**

finely grated **zest** and **juice** of 1 **lime**

2 **eggs**

1¼ cups **self-rising flour**

½ teaspoon **baking powder**

To finish

¼ cup **superfine sugar**

a few drops of **red food coloring**

⅔ cup **heavy cream**

12 **fresh strawberries**

Line a 12-section mini tart pan with paper cake liners. Chop the dried strawberries roughly and put in a small bowl with the tequila. Cover and let soak for at least 2 hours, so that the strawberries plump up.

Drain the strawberries, reserving the tequila. Put the butter, sugar, lime zest, eggs, flour, and baking powder in a bowl and beat with a handheld electric mixer for about a minute, until light and creamy. Stir in the strawberries. Divide the cake mixture between the paper liners.

Bake in a preheated oven, 350°F, for 20 minutes, or until risen and just firm to the touch. Transfer to a wire rack to cool.

Put the sugar in a small bowl and add the food coloring. Work the coloring into the sugar using the back of a teaspoon. Brush the edges of the cakes with a little lime juice and roll the rims in the colored sugar. Mix the remaining lime juice with the reserved tequila. Pierce the cakes all over with a skewer and drizzle over the juice mixture.

Whip the cream until just beginning to hold its shape and pipe or spoon over the cakes. Decorate each with a whole fresh strawberry.

For piña colada cupcakes, omit the strawberries and tequila and make the cake mixture as above, but add ⅓ cup dry flaked coconut to the ingredients before beating, then stir in ½ cup chopped semidried pineapple. Bake as above. Lightly ⅔ cup heavy cream with 3 tablespoons white rum and spoon over the cooled cakes. Decorate with fresh pineapple wedges.

mini minted cupcakes

Makes **50**
Preparation time **45 minutes**,
  plus cooling
Cooking time **12 minutes**

2 oz **extra-strong mints**
  (about 1¼ tubes)
½ cup **lightly salted butter**,
  softened
⅓ cup **superfine sugar**
2 **eggs**
1 cup **self-rising flour**
½ teaspoon **baking powder**

To decorate
3½ oz **bittersweet chocolate**,
  chopped
1 oz **milk chocolate**, chopped

Stand 50 mini paper or foil cake (petit four) liners on a baking sheet. Put the mints in a plastic bag and beat with a rolling pin to break them into a coarse crumb.

Tip the mints into a bowl and add all the remaining cake ingredients. Beat with a handheld electric mixer for about a minute, until light and creamy. Divide the cake mixture between the paper liners.

Bake in a preheated oven, 350°F, for 12 minutes or until risen and just firm to the touch. Transfer to a wire rack to cool.

Melt the bittersweet and milk chocolate in separate bowls (see pages 16–17). Put the melted milk chocolate in a paper piping bag and snip off the tiniest tip (see page 15). Spread the bittersweet chocolate over the cakes. Use the milk chocolate to scribble lines back and forth over the plain chocolate or little dots. Let in a cool place to set before serving.

For mini mint fudge cakes, make the cake mixture as above, but substitute 2 tablespoons cocoa powder for 2 tablespoons of the flour. Bake as above. Melt 7 oz white chocolate with 4 tablespoons milk, stirring until smooth. Stir in 1¼ cups confectioners' sugar. Spread over the cooled cakes and dust with cocoa powder.

frangipane & apricot cupcakes

Makes **12**

Preparation time **30 minutes**,
plus cooling

Cooking time **25 minutes**

¾ cup sliced **dried apricots**

5 tablespoons **brandy**

3 tablespoons **water**

5 tablespoons **apricot jam**

scant ½ cup **almond paste**

confectioners' sugar, for
dusting

½ cup **lightly salted butter**,
softened

⅓ cup **superfine sugar**

2 **eggs**

1¼ cups **self-rising flour**

½ teaspoon **baking powder**

½ cup **ground almonds**

1 teaspoon **almond extract**

Line a 12-section mini tart pan with paper cake liners.
Cook the apricot slices gently in the brandy and water
in a small saucepan for 4–5 minutes, until plumped up
slightly and most of the liquid has been absorbed. Press
the jam through a strainer into the pan and let cool.

Roll out the almond paste on a work surface lightly
dusted with confectioners' sugar. Cut out small heart
shapes using a cutter, about 1 inch in diameter. Gather
the remaining almond paste into a ball. Place the
hearts on a baking sheet lined with parchment paper
and heat under a preheated moderate broiler, watching
closely, until beginning to toast. Let cool.

Put all the remaining ingredients in a bowl. Grate in
the remaining almond paste and beat with a handheld
electric mixer for about a minute, until light and creamy.
Divide between the paper liners.

Bake in a preheated oven, 350°F, for 20 minutes. or
until risen and just firm to the touch. Transfer to a wire
rack to cool.

Pile teaspoonfuls of the apricot mixture onto the cakes
and position a heart on top. Serve dusted with
confectioners' sugar.

For mini linzer cakes, beat together ½ cup softened
lightly salted butter, heaping ½ cup superfine sugar,
1 cup self-rising flour, ½ teaspoon baking powder,
½ cup ground almonds, 2 eggs, and 1 teaspoon almond
extract until light and creamy. Spoon into the paper
liners and bake as above. Once cooled, top each with
1 tablespoon raspberry jam and scatter with toasted
slivered almonds. Dust with confectioners' sugar.

lavender cupcakes

Makes **12**

Preparation time **20 minutes**, plus cooling

Cooking time **20 minutes**

6 **lavender flowers**, plus extra small **sprigs** to decorate
½ cup **lightly salted butter**, softened
heaping ½ cup **superfine sugar**
finely grated **zest** of ½ **orange**
2 **eggs**
1¼ cups **self-rising flour**
½ teaspoon **baking powder**

Icing
1¼ cups **confectioners' sugar**
4–5 teaspoons **orange juice**
a few drops of **lilac food coloring**

Line a 12-section mini tart pan with paper cake liners. Pull the lavender flowers from their stems and put in a bowl with the butter, superfine sugar, orange zest, eggs, flour, and baking powder. Beat with a handheld electric mixer for about a minute, until light and creamy. Divide the cake mixture between the paper liners.

Bake in a preheated oven, 350°F, for 20 minutes, or until risen and just firm to the touch. Transfer to a wire rack to cool.

Mix the confectioners' sugar with enough orange juice in a bowl to make a thin glaze. Color with the food coloring. Spread over the cakes and decorate with small sprigs of lavender flowers.

For sweet thyme cupcakes, finely chop several lemon thyme sprigs. Make the cake mixture as above, but use the lemon thyme in place of the lavender and the finely grated zest of 1 lemon instead of the orange zest. Bake as above. Whip ⅔ cup heavy cream with 2 tablespoons almond-flavored liqueur or honey and spread over the cooled cakes. Decorate with lemon thyme sprigs.

pink rose cupcakes

Makes **12**
Preparation time **20 minutes**,
  plus cooling
Cooking time **20 minutes**

2 cups **sugared rose petals**,
  plus extra to decorate
heaping ½ cup **superfine
  sugar**
½ cup **lightly salted butter**,
  softened
2 **eggs**
1¼ cups **self-rising flour**
½ teaspoon **baking powder**
1 tablespoon **rose water**

Frosting
8 oz **mascarpone cheese**
1 cup **confectioners' sugar**
1 teaspoon **lemon juice**
a few drops of **pink food
  coloring** (optional)

Line a 12-section mini tart pan with paper cake liners. Put the sugared rose petals and superfine sugar in a food processor and process until the rose petals are chopped into small pieces. Tip into a bowl and add all the remaining cake ingredients. Beat with a handheld electric mixer for about a minute, until light and creamy. Divide the cake mixture between the cake liners.

Bake in a preheated oven, (350°F, for 20 minutes, or until risen and just firm to the touch. Transfer to a wire rack to cool.

Beat together the mascarpone, confectioners' sugar, lemon juice, and food coloring, if using, with a wooden spoon in a bowl until smooth. Spread over the tops of the cakes, using a small palette knife and decorate with extra sugared rose petals.

For frosted blueberry cupcakes, put 1 teaspoon egg white in a bowl with ½ cup fresh blueberries and stir until the berries are coated in a thin film of egg white. Roll in a little superfine sugar until coated. Make the cake mixture as above, but omit the sugared rose petals and rose water and add 1 teaspoon vanilla bean paste or vanilla extract. Bake as above. Make the frosting as above, but use a few drops of lilac food coloring instead of the pink food coloring. Spread over the tops of the cooled cakes. Arrange the frosted blueberries on top.

pistachio cream cupcakes

Makes **12**

Preparation time **40 minutes**, plus cooling

Cooking time **20 minutes**

1¼ cups **pistachio nuts**

½ cup **lightly salted butter**, softened

heaping ½ cup **superfine sugar**

2 **eggs**

1¼ cups **self-rising flour**

½ teaspoon **baking powder**

To decorate

⅔ cup **heavy cream**

2 tablespoons **confectioners' sugar**, plus extra for dusting

2 tablespoons **almond-** or **orange-flavored liqueur**

Line a 12-section mini tart pan with paper cake liners. Put the pistachio nuts in a heatproof bowl, cover with boiling water, and let stand for 30 seconds. Drain and rub between several thicknesses of paper towels to loosen the skins. Peel the skins—you don't need to be too thorough, as long as most of the skins are removed. Process in a food processor until finely chopped.

Beat the butter, superfine sugar, eggs, flour, baking powder, and scant ½ cup of the ground nuts with a handheld electric mixer in a bowl for about a minute, until light and creamy. Divide the mixture between the paper liners.

Bake in a preheated oven, 350°F, for 20 minutes, or until risen and just firm to the touch. Transfer to a wire rack to cool.

Peel away the paper liners. Whip the cream with the confectioners' sugar and liqueur in a bowl until only just holding its shape. Transfer half to a separate bowl and reserve. Spread the remainder around the cakes and roll in the remaining ground nuts to coat the sides. Spoon the reserved flavored cream on top.

For macadamia & raspberry cupcakes, finely chop ⅓ cup macadamia nuts and lightly toast in a dry skillet. Let cool. Make the cake mixture as above, but use the macadamia nuts in place of the ground pistachio nuts. Bake as above. Once cooled, split the cakes in half horizontally. Lightly whip ⅔ cup heavy cream with 1 tablespoon confectioners' sugar. Sandwich the cakes together with the cream and fresh raspberries. Serve dusted with confectioners' sugar.

sweet camomile muffins

Makes **12**
Preparation time **15 minutes**
Cooking time **15–18 minutes**

2 tablespooons **camomile tea**
  (either loose leaf or from
  bags)
heaping ¾ cup **ground
  almonds**
scant ½ cup **golden
  superfine sugar**
2¼ cups **all-purpose flour**
1 tablespoon **baking powder**
finely grated **zest** of 1 **lemon**
½ cup **golden raisins**
6 tablespoons **lightly salted
  butter**, melted, plus extra
  to serve
2 **eggs**, beaten
scant 1¼ cups **buttermilk**

Line a 12-section muffin pan with paper muffin liners. Put the tea, ground almonds, and sugar in a food processor and process briefly until combined. Turn into a bowl and stir in the flour, baking powder, lemon zest, and golden raisins.

Mix together the melted butter, eggs, and buttermilk in a separate bowl and add to the flour mixture. Use a large metal spoon to stir the ingredients together until only just combined. Divide the muffin mixture between the paper liners.

Bake in a preheated oven, 425°F, for 15–18 minutes, or until risen and pale golden. Serve warm, split and buttered.

For peppermint tea & white chocolate muffins,
process the ingredients in a food processor as above, but use 2 tablespoons peppermint tea in place of the camomile tea. Mix with the dry ingredients as above, but omit the golden raisins and stir in 3½ oz chopped white chocolate. Combine with the wet ingredients and bake as above.

florentine cupcakes

Makes **12**

Preparation time **20 minutes**,
plus cooling

Cooking time **30 minutes**

sunflower oil, for brushing

¾ cup **slivered almonds**

⅓ cup **golden raisins**

⅔ cup **candied cherries**,
quartered

4 tablespoons **corn syrup**

12 **Vanilla Cupcakes**
(see page 22)

2 oz **bittersweet chocolate**,
broken into pieces

Brush a baking sheet lightly with oil. Beat together the slivered almonds, golden raisins, candied cherries, and corn syrup in a bowl. Tip the mixture onto the prepared baking sheet and spread in a thin layer.

Bake in a preheated oven, 400°F, for 8 minutes, or until the nuts and syrup are turning golden. Remove from the oven and let cool slightly.

Break up the mixture and scatter over the cooled cupcakes in an even layer.

Melt the chocolate (see pages 16–17) and then put in a piping bag fitted with a writing nozzle. Scribble lines of chocolate across the fruit and nut topping. Let stand to set before serving.

For toffee crunch cupcakes, make and bake 12 Chocolate Cupcakes as on page 22. Gently heat ¼ cup unsalted butter, ¼ cup superfine sugar and 2 tablespoons syrup in a small saucepan until the butter has melted. Increase the heat and cook until the mixture starts to turn golden around the edge. Immediately stir in 3½ cups crisp rice cereal and then spoon onto the cakes. Let cool before serving.

red velvet cupcakes

Makes **12**

Preparation time **20 minutes**,
 plus cooling

Cooking time **20–25 minutes**

1¼ cups **self-rising flour**

2 tablespoons **cocoa powder**

½ teaspoon **baking soda**

scant ½ cup **buttermilk**

1 teaspoon vinegar

½ cup **lightly salted butter**,
 softened

scant ½ cup **superfine sugar**

1 egg

⅛ cup peeled and finely grated
 raw beet

Frosting

scant 1 cup **whole-fat cream
 cheese**

2 teaspoons **vanilla extract**

2⅓ cups **confectioners' sugar**

12 **fresh cherries**, to decorate

Line a 12-section muffin pan with paper muffin liners.
Combine the flour, cocoa powder, and baking soda
in a bowl. Mix together the buttermilk and vinegar
in a pitcher.

Beat together the butter and superfine sugar in a
separate bowl until pale and creamy, then beat in the
egg and beet.

Sift half the flour mixture into the bowl and stir in gently
with a large metal spoon. Stir in half the buttermilk
mixture. Sift and stir in the remaining flour mixture, then
the remaining liquid. Divide the muffin mixture between
the paper liners.

Bake in a preheated oven, 350°F, for 20–25 minutes, or
until risen and just firm to the touch. Transfer to a wire
rack to cool.

Beat the cream cheese with a wooden spoon in a
bowl until softened. Beat in the vanilla extract and
confectioners' sugar until smooth. Swirl over the tops
of the cakes and decorate each with a cherry.

For spicy pear & goat' cheese cupcakes, make the
cake mixture as above, but replace the cocoa powder
with an additional 2 tablespoons self-rising flour and
add 1 teaspoon ground allspice, and then omit the
beet. Stir in ½ cup chopped dried pears into the
mixture before baking as above. Beat together ½ cup
soft mild goats' cheese with 1¼ cups confectioners'
sugar and 1 teaspoon lemon juice. Spread over the
tops of the cakes (omit the cherries).

marmalade madeira cupcakes

Makes **12**
Preparation time **15 minutes**
Cooking time **20 minutes**

10 tablespoons **lightly salted butter**, softened
⅓ cup **superfine sugar**
¼ cup **orange marmalade**
2 **eggs**
heaping 1⅓ cups **self-rising flour**
½ teaspoon **baking powder**
1 teaspoon **vanilla extract**
piece of **candied orange peel**

Line a 12-section muffin pan with paper muffin liners. Put the butter, sugar, marmalade, eggs, flour, baking powder, and vanilla extract in a bowl and beat with a handheld electric mixer for about a minute, until light and creamy. Divide the cake mixture between the paper liners.

Cut thin strips from the candied orange peel and lay a couple of slices over each cupcake.

Bake in a preheated oven, 350°F, for 20 minutes, or until risen and just firm to the touch. Transfer to a wire rack to cool.

For ginger spice Madeira cupcakes, make the cake mixture as above, but use ¼ cup ginger marmalade instead of the orange marmalade and add 1 teaspoon ground ginger. Divide the mixture between the paper liners. Thinly slice ⅓ cup preserved ginger pieces and arrange over the cakes before baking as above.

coffee & walnut cupcakes

Makes **12**

Preparation time **20 minutes**, plus cooling

Cooking time **20 minutes**

2 teaspoons **espresso coffee powder**

2 teaspoons **boiling water**

½ cup **lightly salted butter**, softened

heaping ½ cup **superfine sugar**

2 **eggs**

1¼ cups **self-rising flour**

½ teaspoon **baking powder**

heaping ⅓ cup **chopped walnuts**

Coffee buttercream

1 teaspoon **espresso coffee powder**

2 teaspoons **boiling water**

7 tablespoons **unsalted butter**, softened

1¼ cups **confectioners' sugar**

12 **walnut halves**, to decorate

Line a 12-section tart pan with paper cake liners. Blend the coffee powder with the boiling water. Put the butter, superfine sugar, eggs, flour, and baking powder in a bowl. Add the coffee and beat with a handheld electric mixer for about a minute until light and creamy. Stir in the chopped walnuts. Divide the cake mixture between the paper liners.

Bake in a preheated oven, 350°F, for 20 minutes, or until risen and just firm to the touch. Transfer to a wire rack to cool.

Blend the coffee powder with the boiling water for the buttercream. Beat with the butter and confectioners' sugar in a bowl until pale and creamy.

Spread the buttercream over the cakes, using a small palette knife. Alternatively, put in a piping bag fitted with a star nozzle and pipe swirls over the tops of the cakes. Decorate each with a walnut half.

For crunchy peanut cupcakes, beat 6 tablespoons softened lightly salted butter, ½ cup crunchy peanut butter, heaping ½ cup superfine sugar, 2 eggs, 1¼ cups self-rising flour, ½ teaspoon baking powder, and 1 tablespoon milk with a handheld electric mixer for about a minute, until light and creamy. Divide between the paper liners and bake as above. Make the buttercream as above, but omit the coffee powder and water, and spread over the tops of the cooled cakes. Scatter with chopped peanuts.

spiced sweet potato cupcakes

Makes **9**

Preparation time **25 minutes**, plus cooling

Cooking time **35 minutes**

1 small **sweet potato**

10 **cardamom pods**

¼ cup **lightly salted butter**

6 tablespoons **honey**

2 **eggs**, beaten

¾ cup **self-rising flour**

½ teaspoon **baking powder**

3 tablespoons **slivered almonds**, toasted

heaping ⅓ cup **confectioners' sugar**

2 teaspoons **lemon juice**

Line 9 sections of a 12-section mini tart pan with paper cake liners. Scrub the sweet potato and cut into chunks. Cook in a saucepan of boiling water for 10 minutes, or until tender. Drain well and return to the pan. Mash until smooth and let cool.

Crush the cardamom pods in a mortar with a pestle to release the seeds. Discard the shells and crush the seeds as finely as possible.

Melt the butter in a small saucepan with the honey. Turn into a bowl and let cool slightly. Beat in the sweet potato and cardamom, then the eggs, flour, and baking powder.

Divide the cake mixture between the paper liners and scatter with the slivered almonds.

Bake in a preheated oven, 350°F, for 20 minutes, or until risen and just firm. Transfer to a wire rack to cool.

Beat the sugar with the lemon juice in a bowl to make a smooth, thin glaze. Drizzle thin lines of glaze back and forth across the cakes.

For spicy parsnip cakes, make the cake mixture as above, but use heaping ½ cup mashed parsnip instead of the sweet potato and ¼ teaspoon hot chili powder instead of the cardamom. Spoon into the paper liners and scatter with 2 tablespoons pine nuts. Bake as above. Dust lightly with confectioners' sugar before serving.

raspberry amaretti cakes

Makes **12**

Preparation time **20 minutes**, plus cooling

Cooking time **20 minutes**

1 cup broken **amaretti cookies**

⅓ cup packed **light brown sugar**

7 tablespoons **lightly salted butter**, softened

2 **eggs**

⅔ cup **self-rising flour**

½ teaspoon **baking powder**

Topping

scant 1 cup **cream cheese**

½ cup **confectioners' sugar**, plus extra for dusting

2 cups **fresh raspberries**

Line a 12-section mini tart pan with paper cake liners. Put the amaretti cookies in a plastic bag and crush with a rolling pin.

Tip the crushed cookies into a bowl and add the light brown sugar, butter, eggs, flour, and baking powder. Beat with a handheld electric mixer for about a minute, until pale and creamy. Divide the cake mixture between the paper liners.

Bake in a preheated oven, 350°F, for 20 minutes, or until risen and just firm to the touch. Transfer to a wire rack to cool.

Beat the cream cheese with a wooden spoon in a bowl to soften, then beat in the confectioners' sugar. Spread over the tops of the cakes with a small palette knife. Arrange a layer of raspberries on top and dust with confectioners' sugar.

For apricot & almond cupcakes, make the cake mixture as above. Roughly chop ¼ cup dried apricots and ⅓ cup whole blanched almonds and mix together. Scatter about one-third into the cake mixture and lightly stir in, then spoon the mixture into the paper liners. Scatter the remainder over the tops and bake as above. Serve dusted with confectioners' sugar.

lemon meringue cupcakes

Makes **12**

Preparation time **20 minutes**

Cooking time **25 minutes**

½ cup **lightly salted butter**, softened

heaping ½ cup **superfine sugar**

2 **eggs**

1¼ cups **self-rising flour**

½ teaspoon **baking powder**

1 teaspoon **vanilla extract**

finely grated **zest** of 1 **lemon**

Topping & filling

2 **egg whites**

scant ½ cup **superfine sugar**

4 tablespoons **lemon curd**

Line a 12-section tart pan with paper cake liners. Put all the cake ingredients in a bowl and beat with a handheld electric mixer for about a minute, until light and creamy. Divide the cake mixture between the paper liners.

Bake in a preheated oven, 350°F, for 20 minutes, or until risen and just firm to the touch.

Meanwhile, beat the egg whites in a thoroughly clean bowl until peaking. Gradually beat in the sugar, a tablespoonful at a time, to make a firm, glossy meringue.

Remove the cakes from the oven and raise the temperature to 450°F.

Scoop out about 1 teaspoon of sponge from the top of each cake and fill with the lemon curd. Pile up the meringue on top, swirling it with a palette knife. Return to the oven for another 1–2 minutes, watching closely, until the meringue is beginning to brown. Serve warm.

For mini iced Alaskas, make and bake the cakes as above and let cool. Make the meringue as above. Take a small scoop of sponge out of the center of each cake and put ½ teaspoon raspberry or strawberry jam and 1 teaspoon vanilla ice cream into each. Spread the meringue on top so that the ice cream is completely covered. Return to the oven at the raised temperature and lightly brown as above. Serve immediately.

espresso cream cakes

Makes **12**
Preparation time **20 minutes**,
plus cooling
Cooking time **20 minutes**

10 tablespoons **lightly salted
butter**, softened
⅔ cup **superfine sugar**
heaping 1⅓ cups **self-rising
flour**
1 tablespoon **espresso** or
strong coffee powder
3 **eggs**
1 teaspoon **vanilla extract**

To finish
4 tablespoons **coffee-
flavored liqueur**
⅔ cup **heavy cream**
3 oz piece of **bittersweet** or
milk chocolate
cocoa or **drinking chocolate
powder**, for dusting

Line a 12-section mini tart pan with paper cake liners.
Put all the cake ingredients in a bowl and beat with a
handheld electric mixer for 1–2 minutes, until light and
creamy. Divide the cake mixture evenly between the
paper liners.

Bake in a preheated oven, 350°F, for 20 minutes, or
until risen and just firm to the touch. Transfer to a wire
rack to cool.

Drizzle the cooled cupcakes with 2 tablespoons of the
coffee-flavored liqueur.

Put the remaining liqueur in a bowl with the cream and
whip until the cream is thickened and only just holds its
shape. Spread the cream over the tops of the cakes,
using a small palette knife, swirling it right to the edges.

Pare curls from the piece of chocolate, using a
vegetable peeler—if the chocolate breaks off in small,
brittle shards, try softening it in the microwave for a
few seconds first, but be careful not to overheat and
melt it. Scatter the chocolate curls over the cakes and
dust with a little cocoa or drinking chocolate powder.
Store the cakes in a cool place until ready to serve.

For liqueur-drizzled mocha cakes, toast ½ cup
slivered almonds and mix with 1 tablespoon superfine
sugar and ¼ teaspoon ground cinnamon. Make the
cake mixture as above and divide between the paper
liners. Scatter with half the almond mixture and then
bake as above. Drizzle each cake with ½ teaspoon
coffee-flavored liqueur and scatter with the remaining
almond mixture. Return to the oven for 3 minutes, then
transfer to a wire rack to cool.

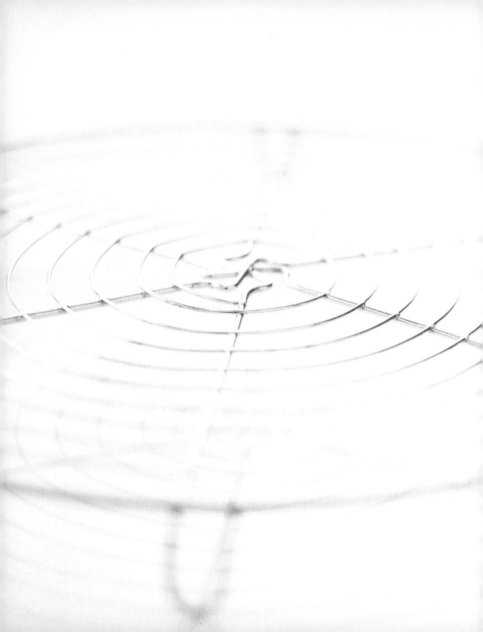

savory
cupcakes

corn, chili & bacon muffins

Makes **12**
Preparation time **15 minutes**,
   plus cooling
Cooking time **25 minutes**

2 **corn on the cobs**
4 **smoked slices bacon**, finely
   chopped
1 small **onion**, finely chopped
2½ cups **cornmeal**
1 tablespoon **baking powder**
½ teaspoon **salt**
1½ teaspoons **crushed
   dried chiles**
1 teaspoon **cumin seeds**,
   crushed
¼ cup chopped **fresh cilantro**
2 **eggs**
5 tablespoons **lightly salted
   butter**, melted
scant 1 cup **milk**

Line a 12-section muffin pan with paper muffin liners.
Cook the corn cobs in a large saucepan of boiling
water for 5 minutes. Drain and let cool. Using a knife,
strip the kernels away from the cobs.

Put the bacon and onion in a small, dry skillet and
cook gently, stirring frequently, until the bacon is
turning crisp and golden. Let cool.

Mix together the cornmeal, baking powder, salt, chiles,
cumin, and cilantro in a bowl. Stir in the bacon, onion,
and corn.

Beat the eggs with the melted butter and milk and add
to the dry ingredients. Use a large metal spoon to stir
the ingredients gently together until only just combined.
Divide the muffin mixture between the paper liners.

Bake in a preheated oven, 425°F, for 15 minutes, or
until risen and pale golden. Serve warm or cold.

For Indian spiced cornbreads, crush 12 cardamom
pods in a mortar with a pestle. Remove and discard
the shells and add 1 teaspoon each of cilantro and
fennel seeds. Grind with the cardamom seeds. Make
the muffin mixture as above, but omit the corn and fry
the seeds in 1 tablespoon vegetable oil with the onion
and 2 finely chopped celery stalks instead of the
bacon. Bake as above.

red pepper & pine nut cupcakes

Makes **12**

Preparation time **20 minutes**,
   plus cooling

Cooking time **30 minutes**

10 tablespoons **lightly salted
   butter**, softened
2 **red bell peppers**, cored,
   seeded and diced
2 **shallots**, thinly sliced
2 **garlic cloves**, crushed
½ cup **pine nuts**
1 cup **all-purpose flour**
2 teaspoons **baking powder**
1⅓ cups **ground almonds**
4 **eggs**, beaten
12 small **bay leaves** (optional)
pepper

Line a 12-section mini tart pan with paper cake liners.
Melt 1 tablespoon of the butter in a skillet and gently
fry the red bell peppers, shallots, and garlic for 5
minutes, until soft. Drain to a plate. Tip the pine nuts
into the skillet and cook for 2–3 minutes, until
beginning to brown. Let cool.

Put the remaining butter in a bowl with the flour,
baking powder, ground almonds, eggs, and plenty of
pepper. Stir well to mix, then stir in the red pepper
mixture and pine nuts. Divide the cake mixture
between the paper liners and push a bay leaf into
the top of each cake, if liked.

Bake in a preheated oven, 350°F, for 20 minutes, or
until risen and just firm. Transfer to a wire rack. Serve
warm or cold.

For artichoke & caper cupcakes, thoroughly drain
a 9 oz jar artichoke antipasta and cut the artichokes
into small pieces. Rinse and drain 2 tablespoons
capers. Make the cake mixture as above, but omit
the bell peppers, shallots, and garlic, reduce the
butter to ½ cup and add the artichokes and capers in
place of the red pepper mixture with the pine nuts.
Bake as above.

goat cheese & tomato cakes

Makes **12**
Preparation time **25 minutes**
Cooking time **15 minutes**

2⅔ cups **all-purpose flour**,
    plus extra for dusting
1 tablespoon **baking powder**
½ teaspoon **salt**
½ teaspoon **dried oregano**
¼ cup **basil**, torn into small
    pieces
2 **scallions**, finely chopped
1 cup **sundried tomatoes**,
    drained and chopped
scant 1¼ cups **buttermilk**
1 **egg yolk**
7 oz **goat cheese**, cut into
    small pieces
milk, for glazing
pepper

Cut out twelve 5-inch squares of nonstick parchment paper and press a square into each section of a 12-section muffin pan. Mix together the flour, baking powder, salt, and oregano in a bowl. Stir in the basil, scallions, and tomatoes.

Mix the buttermilk with the egg yolk, add to the bowl and stir until only just combined, sprinkling in a little more flour if the mixture is very sticky.

Turn out onto a lightly floured work surface and cut into 12 even pieces. Shape each into a ball.
Drop one ball into each of the lined cup sections.

Push your thumb into each ball to create a small cavity in the center and insert a few pieces of goat cheese into each. Brush with milk to glaze. Sprinkle with plenty of pepper.

Bake in a preheated oven, 425°F for 15 minutes, or until risen and beginning to color. Transfer to a wire rack to cool.

For leek & Gruyère cupcakes, roughly chop 1 leek and fry gently in 2 tablespoons lightly salted butter until softened. Mix together the dry ingredients as above, but then add the leek, ¾ cup grated Gruyère cheese, and ½ teaspoon freshly grated nutmeg instead of the basil, scallions and tomatoes. Mix in the wet ingredients and shape into balls as above, but omit the goat cheese. Brush with milk to glaze, season with plenty of pepper, and bake as above.

parmesan & pancetta cupcakes

Makes **9**

Preparation time **20 minutes**,
plus cooling

Cooking time **25–30 minutes**

3½ oz **thinly sliced pancetta**

5 tablespoons **olive oil**

2⅓ cups **self-rising flour**

2 teaspoons **baking powder**

⅔ cup finely grated
Parmesan cheese

scant 1 cup **milk**

1 **egg**, beaten

2 tablespoons **grainy
mustard**

Line 9 sections of a 12-section muffin pan with paper muffin liners. Cut nine 2-inch strips from the pancetta. Finely chop the remainder. Heat 1 tablespoon of the oil in a small skillet and gently fry the pancetta strips for 5 minutes, until turning crisp. Drain to a plate. Fry the chopped pancetta in the pan for 3–4 minutes. Let cool.

Put the flour and baking powder in a bowl. Stir in the Parmesan and chopped pancetta until evenly mixed.

Whisk together the remaining oil, milk, egg, and mustard with a fork in a pitcher and add to the bowl. Stir gently until only just combined.

Divide the muffin mixture between the paper liners and place a strip of pancetta on top of each.

Bake in a preheated oven, 400°F, for 15–20 minutes, or until risen and pale golden. Transfer to a wire rack. Serve warm or cold.

For chorizo & rosemary cupcakes, cut a 3½-oz piece of chorizo sausage into small dice. Fry the chorizo instead of the pancetta strips in the oil as above. Add to the flour and baking powder with the Parmesan, then continue to make the mixture as above, but whisk 2 teaspoons finely chopped rosemary in with the oil, milk, and egg (omit the mustard). Spoon into the paper liners and top each with a rosemary sprig before baking.

smoked salmon cakes

Makes **18**

Preparation time **25 minutes**,
 plus cooling

Cooking time **10 minutes**

1¼ cups **buckwheat flour**

1¼ cups **self-rising flour**

½ teaspoon **baking powder**

3 tablespoons chopped **dill**,
 plus extra sprigs to garnish

2 tablespoons chopped
 parsley

good pinch of **salt**

¼ cup **lightly salted butter**,
 melted

⅔ cup **milk**, plus
 2 tablespoons

2 **eggs**, beaten

1¼ cups **cream cheese**

3½ oz **smoked salmon**

pepper

Line 18 sections of two 12-section mini tart pans with paper cake liners. Put the flours, baking powder, dill, parsley, and salt in a bowl and mix together.

Whisk together the melted butter, the ⅔ cup milk, and the eggs with a fork in a pitcher and pour into the bowl. Using a large metal spoon, gently mix the ingredients together until evenly combined. Divide the mixture between the paper liners so that they are filled about halfway.

Bake in a preheated oven, 400°F, for 10 minutes, or until slightly risen and firm to the touch. Transfer to a wire rack to cool, peeling away the paper liners, if liked.

Beat the cream cheese in a bowl to soften, then beat in the remaining milk. Pipe or spread the mixture over the cakes. Cut the salmon into strips and roll up loosely to resemble flowers. Use to decorate the tops of the cakes. Garnish with dill sprigs and a grinding of pepper.

For malted pepper & herb muffins, rinse and drain 2 tablespoons green peppercorns in brine and lightly crush. Line 8 sections of a 12-section muffin pan with paper muffin liners. Make the mixture as above, but use 1¼ cups malt flour instead of the buckwheat flour and the peppercorns in place of the dill. Bake as above. Beat ⅔ cup cream cheese with 1 tablespoon rinsed, drained, and chopped capers, 4 chopped small gherkins, and 1 tablespoon chopped parsley. Serve with the muffins.

spicy cheese & parsnip muffins

Makes **10**
Preparation time **20 minutes**,
  plus cooling
Cooking time **30 minutes**

1⅔ cups diced **parsnips**
scant 1 cup **milk**
4 tablespoons **olive oil**
1 **egg**, beaten
1 teaspoon **Tabasco sauce**
2 teaspoons **pink**
  peppercorns, crushed
2¼ cups **all-purpose flour**
1 tablespoon **baking powder**
¾ cup finely grated **Gruyère**
  cheese
salt

Line 10 sections of a 12-section muffin pan with
paper muffin liners. Cook the parsnips in a saucepan of
lightly salted boiling water for 10 minutes until tender.
Drain, mash, and let cool.

Beat the milk into the cooled parsnips along with the oil,
egg, Tabasco sauce, and 1 teaspoon of the peppercorns,
adding a dash more milk if the mixture feels dry.

Put the flour, baking powder, ½ teaspoon salt, and all
but 1 tablespoon of the cheese in a large bowl and mix
well. Add the parsnip mixture and stir with a large metal
spoon until the ingredients are only just combined.

Divide the muffin mixture between the paper liners
and sprinkle with the remaining cheese, peppercorns,
and a little extra salt.

Bake in a preheated oven, 425°F, for 20 minutes, or
until risen and pale golden. Transfer to a wire rack.
Serve warm or cold.

For celeriac & mushroom muffins, cook 1⅔ cups
diced celeriac in a saucepan of boiling water until just
tender. Drain and mash well. Thinly slice 7 oz small
mushrooms and fry in 1 tablespoon butter until all the
moisture has evaporated. Let cool. Make the muffin
mixture as above, but use the celeriac mash instead
of the parsnip mash and 1 teaspoon crushed green
peppercorns instead of pink peppercorns, then stir
the mushrooms into the dry ingredients. Once divided
between the paper liners as above, sprinkle with
another teaspoon crushed green peppercorns along
with the remaining cheese and a little extra salt as
above. Bake as above.

pumpkin & red onion cupcakes

Makes **12**
Preparation time **25 minutes**,
  plus cooling
Cooking time **50 minutes–**
  1 hour

1 lb 2 oz **pumpkin** or
  butternut squash
1 **red onion**, sliced
5 tablespoons **olive oil**
2¼ cups **self-rising flour**
scant ½ cup **cornmeal**
1 cup chopped **fresh cilantro**
½ teaspoon **celery salt**
2 teaspoons **baking powder**
3 **eggs**, beaten
⅔ cup **milk**

Line a 12-section muffin pan with paper muffin liners. Cut the pumpkin or squash into small dice, discarding the skin and seeds—you should have about 2¾ cups flesh. Spread out in a roasting pan with the onion slices and drizzle with 1 tablespoon of the oil. Roast in a preheated oven, 425°F, for 30–40 minutes, turning once or twice, until beginning to color. Let cool.

Mix together the flour, cornmeal, cilantro, celery salt, and baking powder in a bowl. Whisk together the eggs, milk, and remaining oil with a fork in a pitcher.

Stir the cooled pumpkin or squash and onion into the dry ingredients. Add the egg mixture and mix together until the ingredients are only just combined. Divide the muffin mixture between the paper liners.

Bake in the oven for 20 minutes, or until risen and just firm. Transfer to a wire rack to cool. Serve warm or cold.

For lentil cakes with crushed spices, thoroughly drain a 13 oz can green lentils. Crush 1 teaspoon each of cilantro, fennel, and cumin seeds in a mortar with a pestle. Make the muffin mixture as above, but use the lentils in place of the roasted vegetables, whisk 1 teaspoon medium curry paste into the egg mixture, and add the spices with the dry ingredients. Bake as above.

mini cheese & chive cakes

Makes **20**
Preparation time **10 minutes**
Cooking time **10–12 minutes**

1⅔ cups **self-rising flour**
1 teaspoon **baking powder**
good pinch of **salt**
½ cup finely grated **sharp Cheddar cheese**,
4 tablespoons snipped **chives**
4 tablespoons **lightly salted butter**, melted
7 tablespoons **milk**
1 **egg**, beaten

Line 20 sections of two 12-section mini muffin pans with mini paper cake liners. Put the flour, baking powder, and salt in a bowl. Stir in the cheese and chives until evenly mixed.

Whisk together the melted butter, milk, and egg with a fork in a pitcher and add to the bowl. Stir well to form a thick paste. Divide the mixture between the paper liners.

Bake in a preheated oven, 400°F, for 10–12 minutes, or until risen and pale golden. Transfer to a wire rack. Serve warm or cold.

For mini Parmesan & olive cakes, chop ½ cup pitted black olives into small pieces and mix with the dry ingredients as above, but use ¼ cup finely grated Parmesan cheese instead of the Cheddar and omit the chives. Continue making the mixture as above, but whisk 1 tablespoon tapenade in with the melted butter, milk, and egg. Bake as above.

rye & caraway muffins

Makes **12**

Preparation time **10 minutes**

Cooking time **20 minutes**

3 tablespoons **molasses**

4 tablespoons **lightly salted butter**, plus extra for greasing

1 **egg**

1 cup **milk**

1¼ cups **rye flour**

1¼ cups **all-purpose flour**

1 tablespoon **baking powder**

½ teaspoon **salt**

2 teaspoons **caraway seeds**

Grease a 12-section muffin pan, preferably nonstick. Put the molasses and butter in a small saucepan and heat gently until the butter has melted. Whisk together the egg and milk with a fork in a pitcher and stir in the treacle and butter.

Put the flours, baking powder, salt, and caraway seeds in a bowl and add the wet ingredients. Stir gently until the ingredients are evenly combined. Divide the mixture between the cup sections in the pan.

Bake in a preheated oven, 425°F, for 15 minutes, or until well risen. Transfer to a wire rack. Serve warm or cold.

For easy Boston muffins, make the mixture as above, but replace ⅔ cup of the all-purpose flour with scant ½ cup whole-wheat flour and ¼ cup cornmeal, omit the caraway seeds, and add ⅓ cup raisins to the dry ingredients. Bake as above.

saffron & potato muffins

Makes **12**
Preparation time **20 minutes**,
plus cooling
Cooking time **25 minutes**

2 cups diced **potatoes**
½ teaspoon crumbled **saffron
strands**
1 tablespoon **boiling water**
scant 1 cup **milk**
4 tablespoons **olive oil**
1 **egg**, beaten
2¼ cups **all-purpose flour**
1 tablespoon **baking powder**
2 teaspoons chopped **thyme**,
plus extra sprigs for
sprinkling
1 teaspoon **sea salt**, plus
extra for sprinkling
egg yolk lightly whisked with
1 teaspoon **water**, for glazing
butter, to serve

Line a 12-section mini tart pan with paper cake liners.
Cook the potatoes in a saucepan of salted boiling
water for 8 minutes or until only just tender. Drain
and let cool.

Mix the saffron with the boiling water in a pitcher and
leave to stand for 5 minutes. Whisk together the saffron
and water, milk, oil, and egg with a fork in a bowl.

Mix together the flour, baking powder, chopped thyme,
and salt in a separate bowl, then stir in the potato.
Add the saffron mixture and mix with a large metal
spoon until evenly combined.

Divide the mixture between the paper liners. Brush the
tops lightly with the egg yolk mixture. Sprinkle with a
little extra salt and scatter with thyme sprigs. Bake
in a preheated oven, 425°F, for 15 minutes, or until
risen and pale golden. Transfer to a wire rack. Serve
warm or cold, split and buttered.

For carrot & cilantro buns, dice 4 medium carrots
and cook in a saucepan of lightly salted boiling water
until just tender. Drain thoroughly. Whisk together the
milk, oil, and egg as above, omitting the saffron and
water, and add 1 teaspoon medium curry paste.
Continue to make the mixture as above, but use
2 tablespoons chopped fresh cilantro in place of the
thyme and stir in the cooked carrots instead of the
potato. Once divided between the paper liners, brush
the tops with the egg yolk mixture, sprinkle with a little
extra salt, and bake as above.

special
occasion
cupcakes

christmas garland

Makes **1 garland of 24 cupcakes**
Preparation time **25 minutes**, plus cooling
Cooking time **20–25 minutes**

6 tablespoons **apricot jam**
1 tablespoon **water**
24 **Cranberry Spice Cupcakes** (see page 22) or **Fruit & Nut Cupcakes** (see page 24)
confectioners' sugar, for dusting
bunch of **red seedless grapes**
bunch of **green seedless grapes**
3–4 **clementines**, halved
3–4 **dried whole figs**, halved
plenty of **bay leaf sprigs**

Press the jam through a strainer into a small saucepan and add the water. Heat gently until softened, then spread in a thin layer over the tops of the cooled cakes.

Arrange 15–16 of the cakes in a staggered circle on a round flat platter or tray, at least 14 inches in diameter. Using a small, fine strainer or tea strainer, dust the cakes on the platter with plenty of confectioners' sugar.

Fold a piece of paper into 4 thicknesses, then cut out a holly leaf shape, about 2½ inches long. Press a holly leaf paper template gently onto the center of 4 more cakes and dust lavishly with confectioners' sugar. Carefully lift off the templates by sliding a knife under the paper to remove them without disturbing the sugar. Repeat on the remaining cakes. Arrange the cakes in a circle on top of the first layer.

Cut the grapes into small clusters. Tuck all the fruits into the gaps around the cakes and into the center of the plate. Finish by arranging small sprigs of bay leaves around the fruits.

For cranberry glazed cupcakes, put 1½ cups fresh cranberries in a small saucepan with ¼ cup superfine sugar, ½ teaspoon ground ginger, 2 tablespoons port, and 1 tablespoon water. Heat gently until the sugar has dissolved, then simmer until the cranberries are soft and beginning to split. Tip into a bowl and let cool. Beat 8 oz mascarpone cheese with 5 tablespoons confectioners' sugar and pipe a little around the edges of the cooled cakes. Pile the cranberry mixture into the centers.

mincemeat cupcakes

Makes **12**

Preparation time **20 minutes**, plus cooling

Cooking time **20–25 minutes**

½ cup **lightly salted butter**, softened

2 tablespoons packed **dark brown sugar**

2 **eggs**

1¼ cups **self-rising flour**

½ teaspoon **baking powder**

1 teaspoon **ground allspice**

1 tablespoon **milk**

scant 1 cup **luxury mincemeat**

Topping

⅔ cup **heavy cream**

4 tablespoons **sherry**

2 tablespoons **confectioners' sugar**

edible pink and silver balls, to decorate

Line a 12-section muffin pan with silver or gold foil muffin liners. Put the butter, brown sugar, eggs, flour, baking powder, allspice, and milk in a bowl and beat with a handheld electric mixer for about a minute, until light and creamy. Add the mincemeat and stir in until evenly mixed. Divide the cake mixture between the foil liners.

Bake in a preheated oven, 350°F, for 20–25 minutes, or until risen and just firm to the touch. Transfer to a wire rack to cool.

Put the cream, sherry, and confectioners' sugar in a bowl and whip until the mixture only just holds its shape. Pile the cream over the cakes and scatter with pink and silver balls to decorate.

For Christmas pudding cupcakes, roll out 2 oz green ready-to-use rolled fondant thinly on a work surface lightly dusted with confectioners' sugar and cut out 24 small holly shapes using a cutter. Roll 36 tiny holly berries from a small piece of red ready-to-use rolled fondant. Transfer to a sheet of wax paper and let stand to harden. Make and bake the cakes as above. Blend 2 tablespoons smooth apricot jam with 2 teaspoons sherry and brush over the tops of the cooled cakes. Roll out 3½ white ready-to-use rolled fondant thinly and cut out small circles with a slightly wavy edge. Arrange on top of the cakes and decorate with the leaves and berries, securing with a dampened paintbrush.

christmas stars

Makes **12**
Preparation time **35 minutes**,
 plus cooling
Cooking time **20 minutes**

3½ oz **white**
 ready-to-use rolled fondant
12 **Vanilla Cupcakes**
 (see page 22)
½ quantity **Buttercream**
 (see page 18)
1⅔ cups **confectioners'**
 sugar,
 plus extra for dusting
4–5 teaspoons **water**
¼ cup **dry flaked coconut**

Knead the white ready-to-use rolled fondant on a work surface lightly dusted with confectioners' sugar. Roll out thickly and cut out small star shapes using a cutter. Transfer to a baking sheet lined with nonstick parchment paper and let stand to harden while decorating the cakes.

Cut out a deep, cone-shaped center from each cooled cake, using a small, sharp knife. Fill each cavity with buttercream and position a cut-out cone on each with the crust side face down.

Mix the confectioners' sugar with the water in a bowl until smooth—the icing should hold its shape but not be too firm. Carefully spread the icing over the tops of the cakes and scatter with flaked coconut.

Gently press a star into the top of each cake and let stand to set.

For winter wonderland cakes, roll out 5 oz white ready-to-use rolled fondant on a work surface lightly dusted with confectioners' sugar and cut out Christmas tree shapes, using small cutters in 2 or 3 different sizes – you need 24 altogether. Transfer to a baking sheet lined with nonstick parchment paper and let stand to harden for several hours or overnight. Make and bake the cakes as above. Beat together 6 tablespoons softened unsalted butter and 1 cup confectioners' sugar until smooth and spread over the cooled cakes. Press the trees gently down into the buttercream. Serve dusted with confectioners' sugar.

snow-covered ginger muffins

Makes **12**
Preparation time **30 minutes**,
  plus cooling & setting
Cooking time **15–20 minutes**

½ cup **lightly salted butter**
½ cup **maple syrup**
⅔ cup packed **light brown sugar**
1¾ cups **self-rising flour**
1 teaspoon **baking powder**
1 teaspoon **ground ginger**
2 **eggs**
½ cup **milk**
3 tablespoons **candied ginger**, chopped, plus extra to decorate

Icing
1⅔ cup **confectioners' sugar**, sifted
4 teaspoons **water**
2 pieces of **candied ginger**, sliced

Line a 12-section mini tart pan with paper or foil cake liners. Put the butter, maple syrup, and brown sugar in a saucepan and heat gently, stirring, until the butter has melted. Mix together the flour, baking powder, and ground ginger in a bowl. Beat together the eggs and milk in a separate bowl.

Take the butter pan off the heat, then beat in the flour mixture. Gradually beat in the egg-and-milk mixture, then stir in the candied ginger. Divide the cake mixture between the cake liners.

Bake in a preheated oven, 350°F, for 10–15 minutes, or until well risen and cracked. Transfer to a wire rack to cool.

Sift the confectioners' sugar into a bowl and gradually mix in the water to create a smooth, spoonable icing. Drizzle random lines of icing from a spoon over the muffins and decorate with slices of candied ginger. Let stand to harden for 30 minutes before serving.

For jewelled Christmas muffins, make the cake mixture as above, but use 6 finely chopped candied cherries instead of the candied ginger. Mix together ½ cup chopped multicolored candied cherries and 2½ tablespoons chopped semidried pineapple. Make the icing as above, spread over the cooled cakes, and scatter with the candied fruit mixture and plenty of edible gold or silver balls.

easter nests

Makes **12**
Preparation time **35 minutes**,
  plus cooling
Cooking time **25 minutes**

1 quantity **Chocolate Fudge
  Frosting** (see page 18)
12 **Chocolate Cupcakes**
  (see page 22)
7 oz **flaked chocolate bars**,
  cut into 1-inch lengths
36 **candy-covered chocolate
  mini eggs**

Spread the chocolate frosting over the tops of the cooled cakes using a small palette knife, spreading it right to the edges.

Cut the short lengths of flaked chocolate bars lengthwise into thin "shards".

Arrange the chocolate shards around the edges of the cakes, pressing them into the frosting at different angles to resemble birds' nests. Pile 3 eggs into the center of each "nest".

For chocolate chestnut cupcakes, make and bake the cakes as on page 22, but add ½ teaspoon ground cinnamon with the cocoa powder to the cake mixture. Pierce the tops of the cooled cakes with a skewer and drizzle each with 1 tablespoon brandy. Beat together ¾ cup chestnut puree and 2 tablespoons brandy. Whip ⅔ cup heavy cream with ¼ cup confectioners' sugar until just peaking. Stir in the chestnut purée and pile on top of the cakes. Sprinkle with chocolate curls.

easter cupcakes

Makes **12**

Preparation time **30 minutes**,
plus cooling

Cooking time **20 minutes**

½ cup **lightly salted butter**,
softened

heaping ½ cup **superfine
sugar**

2 **eggs**

¾ cup **self-rising flour**

½ teaspoon **baking powder**

½ cup **ground almonds**

finely grated **zest** of 1 **lemon**

Frosting

75 g (3 oz) **unsalted butter**,
softened

2¼ cups **confectioners' sugar**

1 teaspoon **vanilla extract**

3–4 tablespoons **lemon juice**

a few drops of **yellow food
coloring**

12 **sugar flowers**, to decorate

Line a 12-section mini tart pan with paper cake liners. Put all the cake ingredients in a bowl and beat with a handheld electric mixer for 1–2 minutes, until light and creamy. Divide the cake mixture between the paper liners.

Bake in a preheated oven, 350°F, for 20 minutes, or until risen and just firm to the touch. Transfer to a wire rack to cool.

Beat together the unsalted butter. 1¼ cups confectioners' sugar and vanilla extract in a bowl until smooth. Place a teaspoonful on top of each cake and mold into a smooth dome, using a knife.

Beat the remaining confectioners' sugar with enough lemon juice in a separate bowl to make an icing that doesn't quite hold its shape. Beat in the food coloring. Place a teaspoonful on top of the buttercream. Ease the icing over the tops of the cakes to cover the buttercream completely. Decorate each cake with a sugar flower.

For festive spice cupcakes, make the cake mixture as above, but use the grated zest of 1 orange and 1 teaspoon ground allspice instead of the grated lemon zest. Bake as above. Make the fondant as above, but use 2–3 tablespoons orange juice in place of the lemon juice and color the icing with a few drops of red food coloring. Spread the icing over the cooled cakes and decorate with whole spices, such as star anise, pieces of cinnamon stick, cardamom pods, and whole cloves.

mini simnel cakes

Makes **12**

Preparation time **30 minutes**, plus cooling & soaking

Cooking time **30 minutes**

½ cup **lightly salted butter**, softened, plus extra for greasing

¼ cup packed **light brown sugar**

1 piece of **preserved ginger** from a jar, finely chopped, plus 2 tablespoons **ginger syrup**

2 **eggs**

1¼ cups **self-rising flour**

½ teaspoon **baking powder**

½ teaspoon freshly grated **nutmeg**

heaping 1 cup **luxury mixed dried fruit**, soaked in 3 tablespoons **brandy** or **orange-flavored liqueur** for 1 hour

scant 1½ cups **white almond paste**

confectioners' sugar, for dusting

Line a 12-section mini tart pan with paper liners. Put the butter, sugar, ginger, eggs, flour, baking powder, and nutmeg in a bowl and beat with a handheld electric mixer for about a minute, until smooth and creamy. Stir in the fruit and any liquid until evenly mixed.

Roll scant ½ cup of the almond paste into a log shape, about 2½ inches long, and cut into 12 slices. Divide half the cake mixture between the liners and level with the back of a teaspoon. Place a paste slice over each. Cover with the remaining mixture.

Bake in a preheated oven, 350°F, for about 25 minutes, until just firm to the touch. Transfer to a wire rack to cool.

Roll out the remaining paste thinly on a work surface lightly dusted with confectioners' sugar. Cut out 12 circles with a 2-inch cookie cutter. Brush the cakes with the ginger syrup and cover each with a paste circle. Flatten a small piece of paste into a thin ribbon and roll up to make a rose. Position on the cake center. Repeat for the remaining cakes. Put on a baking sheet and heat under a moderate broiler, watching closely, until lightly toasted.

For citrus simnel cakes, beat together ½ cup softened lightly salted butter, ⅓ cup superfine sugar, 2 eggs, 3½ oz self-rising flour, ½ teaspoon baking powder, ½ cup ground almonds, and the finely grated zest of 1 orange and 1 lemon. Scatter with scant 1 cup diced almond paste before baking as above. Mix 2 oz fondant with 1–1½ teaspoons lemon juice and drizzle over the cooled cakes.

flying bats

Makes **12**

Preparation time **40 minutes**,
plus cooling & setting

Cooking time **20 minutes**

4 oz **black ready-to-use
rolled fondant**

confectioners' sugar, for
dusting

2 tablespoons **honey**

12 **Vanilla Cupcakes**
(see page 22)

6 oz **orange ready-to-use
rolled fondant**

1 tube of **black decorator
frosting**

selection of tiny **red, orange**
and **yellow candies**

Knead the black ready-to- use rolled icing on a work surface lightly dusted with confectioners' sugar. Roll out thickly and cut out 12 small bat shapes by hand or using a cutter. Transfer to a baking sheet lined with nonstick parchment paper and let stand to harden while decorating the cakes.

Spread ½ teaspoon of the honey over the top of each cooled cake. Roll out the orange fondant thinly and cut out 12 circles using a 2½ inch cookie cutter. Place an orange circle on top of each cake.

Place a bat on top of each cake. Dampen the edge of the orange fondant and pipe a wiggly line of black decorator around the edge. Press the candies gently into the frosting, over the black wiggly line.

For spooky spider cakes, spread each cake with a thin layer of apricot or red fruit jam. Roll out 7 oz green or blue ready-to-use rolled fondant thinly on a work surface lightly dusted with confectioners' sugar and cut out 12 circles using a 2½-inch cookie cutter. Position one on each cake. Using a tube of black decorator frosting, pipe small spiderswebs onto each cake. Decorate with jelly "bug" candies.

stars, polka dots & stripes

Makes **12**

Preparation time **40 minutes**, plus cooling

Cooking time **20 minutes**

½ quantity **Buttercream** (see page 18)

12 **Vanilla Cupcakes** (see page 22)

5 oz **white ready-to-use rolled fondant**

4 oz **blue ready-to-use rolled fondant**

confectioners' sugar, for dusting

Spread the buttercream in a thin layer over the tops of the cooled cakes, using a small palette knife.

Knead the fondants on a work surface lightly dusted with confectioners' sugar. Take one-third of the white fondant, roll out thinly, and cut out 4 circles using a 2½-inch cookie cutter. Cut out 6 small stars from each round using a cutter. Roll out a little of the blue fondant thinly and cut out 24 stars. Fit the blue stars into each white circle and transfer to 4 of the cakes.

Roll out another one-third of the white fondant thinly. Roll tiny balls of blue fondant between your finger and thumb. Press at intervals onto the white fondant. Gently roll with a rolling pin so that the blue fondant forms dots. Cut out 4 circles and transfer to 4 more cakes.

Cut long strips ¼ inch wide from the remaining blue and white fondants and lay them together on the work surface. Roll lightly with a rolling pin to flatten and secure them together, then cut out 4 more circles. Place on top of the remaining 4 cakes.

For star & moon cupcakes, make and bake 12 Chocolate Cupcakes (see page 22). Melt 3½ oz white chocolate (see pages 16–17). Draw 6 star and 6 moon shapes onto nonstick parchment paper, using 2–2½-inch cutters as guides. Put the chocolate into a paper piping bag (see page 15) and use to fill the shapes. Let stand to set. Melt 3½ oz bittersweet chocolate with 1 tablespoon unsalted butter and spread over the cakes. Peel the paper away from the shapes and position on the cakes.

firework sparklers

Makes **12**
Preparation time **40 minutes**,
    plus cooling & setting
Cooking time **25–30 minutes**

3½ oz **butternut squash**,
    peeled and seeded
½ cup **lightly salted butter**,
    softened
¼ cup packed **light brown
    sugar**
½ cup **honey**
2 **eggs**
1¼ cups **self-rising flour**
⅔ cup **rolled oats**
½ teaspoon **baking powder**
1 teaspoon **ground allspice**

To decorate
2 oz **orange ready-to-use
    rolled fondant**
2 oz **white ready-to-use
    rolled fondant**
1⅔ cups **confectioners'
    sugar**, plus extra for dusting
2 tablespoons **orange juice**
4 tablespoons **orange curd**
indoor sparklers

Line a 12-section mini tart pan with paper or foil cake liners. Grate the squash into a bowl and add all the remaining cake ingredients. Beat with a handheld electric mixer for about a minute, until light and creamy. Divide the cake mixture between the paper or foil liners.

Bake in a preheated oven, 350°F, for 25–30 minutes, or until just firm to the touch. Transfer to a wire rack to cool.

Roll out the orange and white fondants on a work surface lightly dusted with confectioners' sugar and cut out small star shapes, either by hand or using a cutter. Push a wooden toothpick into each and place on a sheet of wax paper to harden for at least an hour.

Beat the confectioners' sugar in a bowl with 2 tablespoons orange juice, adding a little extra juice if necessary to give a thick but spreadable consistency. Spoon over the cakes, spreading to the edges. Take a teaspoon of the orange curd and pour it, in a loose spiral, over each cake. Push a fondant star down into each cake. Just before serving, position the sparklers on the cakes and light.

For honey-drizzled spice cakes, make the cake mixture as above, but use 2 teaspoons ground allspice and add ½ teaspoon ground cinnamon. Bake as above and let cool. Beat scant 1 cup whole-milk yogurt with 1 tablespoon honey and spread over the cakes. Drizzle with extra honey to decorate.

wedding cupcakes

Makes **12**
Preparation time **30 minutes**,
   plus cooling
Cooking time **20 minutes**

12 **Vanilla Cupcakes**
   (see page 22)
4 tablespoons **sherry** or
   orange-flavored liqueur
   (optional)
1⅔ cups **confectioners'**
   sugar, sifted
1–2 tablespoons **lemon juice**
36 **sugared almonds**
12 **frosted flowers**
   (see page 228)
fine white ribbon, to decorate

Drizzle the cakes with the sherry or liqueur, if using. Mix the confectioners' sugar with 1 tablespoon of the lemon juice in a bowl. Slowly add the remaining lemon juice, stirring well with a wooden spoon, until the icing holds its shape but is not difficult to spread—you may not need all the juice.

Spread the lemon-flavored icing over the tops of the cooled cakes, using a small palette knife and arrange 3 sugared almonds in the center of each.

Place a frosted flower on top of each cake and tie a length of white ribbon around each paper cake liner to decorate it, finishing it with a bow.

For big birthday cupcakes, roll out 3½ oz ready-to-use rolled fondant in the color of your choice and stamp out appropriate numbers using cutters. Transfer to a tray lined with nonstick parchment paper and let stand to harden for several hours or overnight. Make and bake the Vanilla Cupcakes as on page 22, but substitute 2 oz grated white chocolate for ¼ cup superfine sugar in the cake ingredients. Melt 3½ oz chopped white chocolate with 5 tablespoons unsalted butter and 2 tablespoons milk in a saucepan, stirring until smooth. Turn into a bowl, beat in ¾ cup confectioners' sugar, and continue beating with a wooden spoon until softly peaking. Spread over the cooled cakes, then gently arrange the fondant numbers, vertically, on top of the cakes and scatter with sugar sprinkles.

valentine hearts

Makes **12**

Preparation time **30 minutes**,
   plus cooling

Cooking time **20 minutes**

1⅔ cups **confectioners'
   sugar**, plus extra for dusting

4–5 teaspoons **rose water**
   or **lemon juice**

12 **Vanilla Cupcakes**
   (see page 22)

3½ oz **red ready-to-use
   rolled fondant**

6 tablespoons **strawberry jam**

Put the confectioners' sugar in a bowl and add
4 teaspoons of the rose water or lemon juice. Mix
until smooth, adding a little more liquid if necessary,
until the icing forms a thick paste. Spread over the
tops of the cooled cakes.

Knead the red fondant on a work surface lightly
dusted with confectioners' sugar. Roll out thickly and
cut out 12 small heart shapes, using a cutter. Place a
heart on the top of each cake.

Press the jam through a small strainer to remove any
lumps. Put the strained jam in a small piping bag fitted
with a writing nozzle. Pipe small dots into the fondant
around the edges of each cake and pipe a line of jam
around the edge of each heart.

For frosted fruit & flower cakes, whip ⅔ cup heavy
cream with 3 tablespoons orange-flavored liqueur
in a small bowl and spread over the cooled cakes.
Scatter with a selection of fresh raspberries, small
red seedless grapes, and fresh blueberries, and
position a small red rose on top of each. Serve
dusted with confectioners' sugar.

frosted flower cupcakes

Makes **12**

Preparation time **40 minutes**,
   plus cooling & setting

Cooking time **20 minutes**

selection of small **edible
   spring flowers**, such as
   primroses, violets, or rose
   petals, or **herb flowers**

1 **egg white**

superfine sugar, for dusting

1 quantity **White Chocolate
   Fudge Frosting**
   (see page 18)

12 **Vanilla Cupcakes**
   (see page 22)

fine pastel-colored ribbon, to
   decorate (optional)

Make sure the flowers are clean and thoroughly dry
before frosting. Put the egg white in a small bowl and
beat lightly with a fork. Put the sugar in a separate bowl.

Using your fingers or a soft paintbrush, coat all the
petals on both sides with the egg white. Dust plenty of
sugar over the flowers until evenly coated. Transfer to
a sheet of nonstick parchment paper and let to stand
for at least 1 hour, until firm.

Spread the chocolate frosting over the tops of the
cooled cakes, using a small palette knife. Decorate the
top of each with the frosted flowers. Tie a length of
ribbon around each paper cake liner to decorate,
finishing it with a ribbon bow, if using.

For coconut frosted cakes, make and bake the
Vanilla Cupcakes as on page 22, but add the finely
grated zest of 2 limes and 1 tablespoon lime juice
to the cake ingredients along with ½ cup dry flaked
coconut. Add 2 teaspoons lime juice and scant
2½ cups confectioners' sugar. Whisk until thick and
smooth, then spread over the cooled cakes. Decorate
with grated lime zest.

tee-off cakes

Makes **12**

Preparation time **40 minutes**, plus cooling

Cooking time **20–25 minutes**

8 tablespons **chocolate hazelnut spread** or ½ quantity **Chocolate Fudge Frosting** (see page 18)

12 **Vanilla** or **Chocolate Cupcakes** (see page 22)

7 oz **green ready-to-use rolled fondant**

confectioners' sugar, for dusting

3 oz **white ready-to-use rolled fondant**

12 **foil-wrapped chocolate golf balls**

Beat the chocolate spread or frosting to soften it slightly, then spread it over the tops of the cooled cakes, using a small palette knife.

Knead the green icing on a work surface lightly dusted with confectioners' sugar. Roll out thinly and cut out 12 circles using a 2-inch cookie cutter. Place a green circle on top of each cake.

Shape 12 small golf tees from the white ready-to-use rolled fondant. Lay one on top of each cake, securing with a dampened paintbrush. Press a foil-wrapped chocolate golf ball into the fondant, alongside the tee, to finish.

For football cupcakes, make the cakes as above and spread with chocolate fudge frosting. Beat 1¼ cups confectioners' sugar in a bowl with a little green food coloring and enough cold water, about 3–4 teaspoons, for the icing to hold its shape but remain spreadable. Spoon a little icing over each cake and spread slightly to the edges so the chocolate frosting still shows through. Position a foil-wrapped chocolate football on top of each cake.

daisy celebration cupcakes

Makes **24**

Preparation time **1−1½ hours**, plus cooling & setting

Cooking time **25 minutes**

1 cup **lightly salted butter**, softened

heaping 1 cup **superfine sugar**

4 **eggs**

1 tablespoon **vanilla bean paste** or **vanilla extract**

finely grated **zest** of 2 **lemons**

heaping 2⅓ cups **self-rising flour**

1 teaspoon **baking powder**

To decorate

confectioners' sugar, for dusting

4 oz **pale pink ready-to-use rolled fondant**

4 oz **deep pink ready-to-use rolled fondant**

1¼ cups **heavy cream**

10 oz **white chocolate**, chopped into small dice

Line two x 12-section mini tart pans with paper cake liners. Put all the cake ingredients in a bowl and beat with a handheld electric mixer for about a minute, until light and creamy. Divide the cake mixture between the paper liners.

Bake in a preheated oven, 350°F, for 20 minutes, or until just firm to the touch—the cakes on the lower oven shelf may need a little longer, but don't swap the pans halfway through cooking or the cakes could sink. Transfer to a wire rack to cool.

Roll out the pale pink fondant thinly on a work surface lightly dusted with confectioners' sugar. Stamp out 12 flower shapes using a cutter about 1¾ inches in diameter. Cup each flower slightly in the palm of your hand and transfer to a sheet of crumpled foil to harden. Roll out the deep pink fondant and make 12 more flowers. Take a tiny piece of pale pink fondant from the trimmings and press against a piece of tuille until the netting leaves an impression in the fondant. Peel away the tuille. Press the fondant gently into the center of a deep pink flower. Repeat for the remaining flowers, alternating the pinks.

Put scant 1 cup of the cream in a small saucepan and bring almost to a boil. Pour over the chocolate in a bowl and leat stand until it has melted, stirring occasionally until smooth. Leave to cool.

Stir the remaining cream into the chocolate mixture and whip until just holding its shape—don't overwhip or the mixture will start to separate. Pipe or spoon over the cakes. Decorate with the prepared flowers.

index

acknowledgments

Executive Editor: Eleanor Maxfield
Senior Editor: Lisa John
Deputy Creative Director: Karen Sawyer
Designer: Geoff Fennell
Photographer: David Munns
Home Economist: Joanna Farrow
Props Stylist: Liz Hippisley
Production Controller: Carolin Stransky

Special photography: © Octopus Publishing Group Limited/David Munns.

Other photography: © Octopus Publishing Group Limited 20; /Stephen Conroy 16 right, 123; /Vanessa Davies 33, 135, 137; /David Munns 68, 142, 180, 202; /Lis Parsons 49, 131, 211; /Gareth Sambidge 8, 25, 31, 39, 46, 71, 77, 83, 91, 101, 107, 111, 115, 119, 127, 141, 165, 179, 205, 209, 213, 219, 221, 225, 227, 231; /Ian Wallace 16 left, 95, 103.